Matt Rudd is senior writer at the *Sunday Times*, which he joined in 2002. His award-winning column, Man Trouble, appears in the *Sunday Times Magazine*. His debut novel, *William Walker's First Year of Marriage: A Horror Story*, was published in 2009, followed a year later by *William's Progress*. His first non-fiction book, *The English: A Field Guide*, was published in 2014.

Praise for *Man Down*

'This is the most honest, most revealing – and funniest – exploration of male mental health I have ever read'
Adam Kay, bestselling author of *This is Going to Hurt*

'There are few people who understand men, or, indeed, unhappy men, more than Matt Rudd. I read everything he writes and this book is essential'
Sathnam Sanghera

'Matt Rudd may have written the most important book in a generation. It could also be the saving grace of millions of young men in their 20s and 30s, getting to them in time before they reach middle age, exhausted, confused and angry, literally saving lives'
Idle Society

'Touchingly honest, and extremely funny ... this is a whole-hearted and important attempt to analyse what has gone wrong for so many men and to make some tentative suggestions for what may help'
The Times

'The brave, funny and searing tale of a man who has it all and is figuring out what went wrong. I loved it'
Christine Armstrong, author of *The Mother of All Jobs*

'I love everything Matt Rudd has ever written'
Chris Evans

'Engaging, sensible and worth reading'
Jake Kerridge, *Sunday Express*

MAN DOWN

Why Men Are Unhappy and What We Can Do About It

MATT RUDD

PIATKUS

PIATKUS

First published in Great Britain in 2020 by Piatkus
This paperback edition published in Great Britain in 2022 by Piatkus

1 3 5 7 9 10 8 6 4 2

A CIP catalogue record for this book
is available from the British Library.

ISBN 978-0-349-42482-8

Typeset in Sabon by M Rules
Printed and bound in Great Britain by
Clays Ltd, Elcograf S.p.A

Papers used by Piatkus are from well-managed forests
and other responsible sources.

Piatkus
An imprint of
Little, Brown Book Group
Carmelite House
50 Victoria Embankment
London EC4Y 0DZ

An Hachette UK Company
www.hachette.co.uk

www.littlebrown.co.uk

NOTE: some names and details of interviewees
and individuals have been changed to protect their privacy.

To Freddie, Felix and Eli

Contents

Introduction

t is 3.20 in the morning and I am wide awake. If I was at a rave or the start of a new relationship, this would be great, but I'm married and middle-aged and this is not great. The bedroom is silent but for the sounds of light sleeping next to me. I have spent many nights lying here thinking I'd prefer it if she had a real foghorn of a snore. At least then I would have some cover to fidget myself back to sleep. Instead, it's like lying next to the Predator. Yes, it's asleep at the moment and I am safe, but if I move at all, it will sense my presence and strike. 'Stop fidgeting,' it will hiss. So I lie there trying not to move, but not trying too hard because the Predator can also sense that. I am completely alone with my thoughts and, in the darkness, those thoughts do not make good company.

Out of necessity, the insomnia I suffered as a teenager came to an end with fatherhood but then returned some time after my fortieth birthday, triggered by just the same things: anxiety, stress ... fear. What could I possibly have to be fearful of? I am a middle-class, white-collar man. The nearest I've come to the breadline is the Saturday morning queue for sourdough. I am privileged and healthy.

This is 2017-ish – two or three years and a lifetime ago. Coronavirus is just a fancy way of saying head cold. The whole world has yet to be upended by pandemic. We have still to experience the grim paint-drying months of social isolation, stalked by spiralling death tolls, wishing we'd made more of our pre-Covid-19 freedoms. I have no idea that I will spend 2020 applauding my own wife off to her hospital each morning and then phoning my aged parents to check they have not developed a 'new and persistent' cough.

But in this golden age of Caligulan extravagances, like the cinema, Nando's and catching a bus, I have still managed to find lots of things to be fearful of. I fear that I am a bad – or at least an absent – parent. I fear that I am a bad husband, too caught up in the parenting I don't do enough of or the work I do too much of to give enough thought to the most important relationship in my life. I fear that I am a negligent son and brother, too caught up in the immediate family I also neglect. I know that I am a misanthrope, slowly retreating from meaningful human connection because I am too busy not having enough time for work or life to be anything as profligate as sociable. I suspect that I am an unsuccessful writer, no longer the next big thing and certainly not the current big thing.

In a discussion six months ago about which foreign correspondent should be commissioned to write a particular think piece, an editor dismissed one suggestion with: 'Oh no, he's over the hill.' The 'he' in question was – and still is – three years younger than me. I replay that scene most nights at 3.23 a.m. I fear that I am older than I am young.

The latest symptom of midlife, to which the sleep deprivation undoubtedly contributes, is an intermittent but profound sense of desolation. It strikes not only in the dead of night but also at random times during the day – on a diverted commuter train, in an uncontained work meeting, in a corridor after a particularly trying call with a broadband provider. The desolation begins with more immediate emotions – anger, frustration, exasperation – but then develops into helplessness and panic. I have to sit down and wait for the panic to subside into more manageable existential resignation – if I can't even get the Wi-Fi to work, what is the point of anything?

On turning sixty, my much-missed colleague AA Gill was pleased to be 'over the meridian of our vital parabola', relieved that he was now far from forty – 'an insipid and insecure age'. I think about that a lot and wish I could be more secure and more whatever the opposite of insipid is. After all, I'm doing all right. I still have a job in the profession I chose. I am still happily married. I have three usually lovely sons who now stay up late enough for me to see them in the evenings. It's all – technically – good. I should be the last person to complain. Except, over the last few years, something has changed. Whatever that thing is, it has changed gradually, imperceptibly, like the hour hand on a relentless clock.

Memory is unreliable, but when I think back to how I felt a decade ago, it was definitely different. I was closer to thirty than forty. Fifty was another island altogether. At work, I was climbing the career ladder at my newspaper, never stopping to look back down or consult the ladder's health-and-safety manual. I clocked up long hours and felt pleased that there were long hours up which to clock. I loved the pressure of the newsroom. I loved deadlines.

'I'll be late tonight, darling,' I used to call home and announce. 'Bit of a crisis.' Remembering this cringing self-importance now makes me blush. By the end of each week, I was exhausted – nodding off in a child's bed after three pages of *The Faraway Tree* and one glass of wine.

'Daddy, finish the chapter.'

But this imbalance was all worth it because I was climbing the ladder. And if I got bored of that ladder, there were always other ladders. Even in that deluded state of youthful confidence, I could accept that I'd left it too late to be a rock star or a lower-division goalkeeper. But there were other professions. For a long time, I kept an article by an ex-journalist I knew who had retrained as a barrister. It had taken her five years and a whole extra mortgage, but there she was in her wig and robes, looking understandably pleased with her legally qualified self.

'It's never too late to swap careers,' read the photo caption. And she was five years older than me.

Now, though, the idea of retraining as a lawyer seems financially, logistically, emotionally and academically bonkers. After taking a weekend course in plumbing and then using what I had learnt to fix a tap in a way that would have guaranteed top billing on *Rogue Traders*, that's out too. My career options have narrowed to the point where it no longer feels like there are any. More bafflingly, this narrowing is all entirely theoretical. I have no idea what would happen if I looked up my old careers adviser. It might go brilliantly. The chap might look at my CV – 'clean driver's licence, proficient at Excel, Malaysia Travel Writer of the Year 2001' – and come up with all manner of alternative arrangements.

'They're looking for more mature bomb-disposal experts . . . I see here you do an excellent lasagne. Have you considered catering? . . . I know a company in Barbados that needs a tall person to look after their flower boxes.'

But in my heart of hearts I know I'm set. I'm stuck. I'm an old dog with non-transferable tricks. And I'm not the only one: more than half of men in management positions are 'unhappy' in their careers and 'would like to change'. But only a very small fraction of them ever do. Despite all manner of sharp- and shiny-toothed recruitment experts queuing up to tell midlifers that 'it's never too late to find the career you love', there are risks. So you have to be brave. You have to be prepared to abandon the status you've achieved and start again. Which would be fine if we were on our own, but, on the whole, we're not.

'Kids, Daddy is going to spend the next twelve months finding himself. Then he's going to spend another three years learning to do the thing he has suddenly decided he always wanted to do. In the meantime, you're all going to have to eat Spam and get paper rounds.'

Most of the self-help gurus writing books and posting YouTube videos on how to turn your life around begin with a story about how they were stuck in a job they didn't enjoy. Then, using their clever, trademarked process, which usually involves some light Buddhism and a life-changing pet/holiday/protein supplement, they transformed themselves. The trouble is, they've all transformed themselves into self-help gurus. As second careers go, it's deeply cynical. We can't all become people whose second career is telling people how easy it is to have a second career.

Inevitably, then, it's back to the first ladder. Except I haven't gone up any rungs lately. That wasn't a conscious decision. It just kind of happened and, on the one hand, it is a relief. In my experience, people at the top of the ladders are even more stressed, miserable and insecure than everyone beneath them. On the other hand, it's not easy just hanging out on a particular rung. People don't like it. If you're not climbing up or sliding down, then you're just getting in the way. You could jump. Every single man I've interviewed has fantasised at one time or another about jumping. I've had whole evenings discussing variations on 'The Escape Plan'. A mortgage-free hovel in France. A small wood in Wales. Why don't we all club together and live communally in Shropshire? Self-sufficiency. The good life. Chickens. It takes as long as the zigzag home to be reminded, often quite forcefully, by our loved ones, that the plan is unworkable. What about school? What about friends? What about the travel-sick dog? When, in more hysterical moments, I suggest to the family that we should all get out of the rat race and live by a loch/in a yurt/ on a longboat/underneath a bridge, my two younger boys give me the midlife-crisis eye roll. The eldest just texts me a midlife-crisis eye-roll emoji.*

---

* That's a lie. He is fourteen and doesn't use anything as Victorian as texting.

So, on we go. Eat. Sleep. Work. Repeat. Eat. Sleep. Work. Oh God! Repeat. Doing – not thinking – until 3.20 a.m., when there is no more doing to do and I wish there wasn't any thinking. And the worry sets in and I just lie there, encircled by worst-case scenarios.

What if I lose my job? What if I can't pay the mortgage? Why haven't I got mortgage insurance? Shall I get out of bed and arrange mortgage insurance? If I do, will I still be able to afford the mortgage? Shall I just go back to sleep? Because what if I'm so tired that I lose my job? And then how will I pay the mortgage? I should definitely get mortgage insurance.

'Stop fidgeting,' hisses the Predator.

In those small, dragging hours, I am miserable. There are no limits to how sorry I can feel for myself. I should not feel sorry for myself. I should not be so self-indulgent. It is pathetic and I hate myself for it. Which makes it worse.

A year and another lifetime ago, I decided to do something about my midlife doldrums. I could have taken up yoga or cross stitch or driving – okay, renting – a red convertible, but instead I started asking other men how they felt. I deliberately sought out those who are, by most definitions, doing fine. Not the full-on one percenters – don't worry, they're miserable too – but certainly 'successful'. They are all earning above-average salaries in decent jobs. They are paying off unfeasible mortgages on overpriced family homes. They are (mostly) happily married fathers of 2.4 children. I decided to focus on them because, if they aren't happy, who is? I thought I would discover their secrets to success, adopt their tips for happiness and stop being such a grump. The problem is that, with one or two exceptions – who may or may not be living in denial – these successful men are not happy. More striking still, most of them admit that they very rarely think about their own happiness.

'I can't,' says one. 'If I start worrying about the meaning of life, I'll go mad. I just have to keep going.'

The stereotype that men don't talk about their feelings is true only up to a point. If you sit them down and explain that you want to have a proper conversation about happiness, it is remarkable how quickly the defences come down. Take the fifty-year-old oil industry consultant who, when asked how much he loves his job, says, 'I don't love it; I tolerate it. It is a means to an end.' Would he still do it if money were no object? 'Fuck no,' he replies. 'I spend long, stressful days working for people I don't always like. My main goal now is survival rather than success. Yes, I have benefited from working in a male-dominated industry, but I am the provider. I have to provide. I definitely live for the weekends.'

Another classic commuter, a forty-three-year-old with three daughters, explains that his priorities changed when he became a father. Previously, he had cared about his pinstripe City job – the next promotion, the next bonus, impressing his boss. But, 'as soon as my first daughter was born, I was looking for ways to get through the day quicker. I was no longer first one in, last one out of the office. It just wasn't important.'

Absolutely no surprise there, of course. Fatherhood does rather change your perspective. But ten years on, his attempts to find a better balance between work and life have failed. 'We moved even further out of London to get the extra bedroom,' he says. 'So now I leave the house before the kids are awake. I get home after the two youngest have gone to bed. Sometimes I'm home in time to see my eldest, but I've noticed that "daddy time" – in the evenings and at the weekends – has this special pressure. I have expectations and my daughters have expectations, too. Those expectations nearly always clash, then they feel disappointed and I feel like a failure.'

His problems pale in comparison to the forty-year-old financial consultant who lives in Hampshire and describes his four-hour commute as 'like being psychologically waterboarded'. He points out that he avoids subjects such as personal happiness because 'I worry I might implode. Superficially, my job is high-profile and rewarding. My family doesn't want for anything. My job is valuable and valued. My competitive drive, paired with a crippling anxiety that everything will implode on Thursday and I will be fired, keeps my feet firmly anchored to the floor.'

Crippling anxiety aside, so far so good. Then, inevitably, comes the but.

'Most working days are long and the stress is relentless. I never take lunch and regularly forget to eat anything until four in the afternoon. Most worryingly, the demands of my particular job now encroach into my consciousness during evenings and weekends. I've stopped seeing my friends, I hardly speak to my family – I have a powerful aversion to the phone at home now – and I simply don't plan anything.' He insists his weekends in Hampshire with his beloved family are great, but they get a lesser version of him: 'I'm jaded, preoccupied and guilty. I do the most ridiculous things to carve out some quiet time. I hide in the bath and go to the cinema on my own.'

A few weeks before our interview, he had felt unwell in a meeting. His doctor had already warned him about stress, told him his blood pressure was far too high and advised him to take some time off. He had ignored that advice, so there he was, room spinning, chest tightening, stars circling. Rather than ask for help, he struggled through the meeting and spent the rest of the day wondering 'if I had got away with it'.

'How I feel is utterly irrelevant,' he says, sensing some explanation is necessary. 'It is irrelevant because I am neck-deep in financial commitments. Mortgages and school fees are not just vanities. In our case they are born out of necessity – two of my children have additional needs. I find myself in a position today where the need to earn a certain amount of money is non-negotiable. This is not where I wanted to be.'

On paper, these men have done everything right. They've ticked all the boxes young men are told to tick: they've established careers, settled down, had kids, accumulated all the stuff to which we are indoctrinated to aspire. House. Car. Nespresso machine. Most importantly, they are not women. That is quite the advantage. They are men in a man's world. They are dads. Imagine if they had been mums.

For years, mums have been told, usually by top female executives with a fleet of nannies and enough spare time ... to ... write ... a ... book, that they can 'have it all'. All they have to do is lean in and it's easy to raise two, three, eight kids while wowing everyone in the boardroom. If they end up crying with exhaustion over the packed lunches at 5.30 a.m. because they dropped their Blackberry in the bath at midnight and they're supposed to be hosting a conference call with Japan at eight, then that's just because they didn't lean in enough.* The net result of all this pressure is that working mums can feel guilty when they're at work *and* guilty when they're at home. Double guilt. Guilt squared. Genius.

By comparison, working fathers have it easy. The implication, spoken and unspoken, is that they – *we* – have the best of both worlds. And, on the surface, that's true. Life *is* easier for men. We still get paid more for doing the same jobs. We are still 40 per cent more likely than women to be promoted to management roles. Hurrah! Even in families where both parents work, most of the emotional labour – supporting the children, organising the diary, scheduling play dates and parties, the vipers' nest that is the PTA – is still done by women. Men do washing-up and petrol, wine and bins. Women do everything else. It's all very 1950s.

Scrape beneath the surface, though, and the myth of the easy male life starts to unravel. The most recent Samaritans Suicide Statistics Report shows that men in the UK are three times more likely to take their own lives than women. And those aged between 45 and 49 have the highest rate

---

* Read Christine Armstrong's excellent *Mother of All Jobs* to understand exactly how much pressure modern working women are under to meet the ideal that is sold in their particular section of the self-help library. Or simply ask any working woman.

of all – nearly four times that of women of the same age. Analysis by the Office for National Statistics shows that middle-aged people have the lowest levels of personal well-being, reporting high levels of anxiety and low levels of happiness and life satisfaction. And middle-aged men are even less happy and less satisfied than their unhappy, unsatisfied female counterparts. The evidence is clear and deeply ironic: the system set up by men, for men, isn't working for the vast majority of men.

The psychologist Elliott Jaques coined the term 'midlife crisis' in 1965 while trying to understand why creative geniuses stopped being quite so creative – or genius – when they hit their mid-thirties. The term languished in relative obscurity for more than a decade until Gail Sheehy used it in her 1976 *New York Times* best-seller *Passages: Predictable Crises of Adult Life*. Her descriptions of various couples running into the doldrums at a certain, middling age struck a chord with millions. Finally, an explanation. Finally, a useful little label. If and when a man flames out at work, blows up his marriage or goes the full Michael Douglas and shoots up a fast-food joint at 10.32 in the morning, it is because of his midlife crisis. It's an age thing. It's a loss of virility thing. It's a sudden realisation of your own mortality thing. We're all going to die and I can't even get a McMuffin when I want a McMuffin.

Ever since then, the midlife crisis has been the punchline to a joke. It is the perennial sitcom character who swapped his self-awareness for a much younger model. Haha, he bought a sports car. Haha, he got a comb-over. Haha, he thinks he still looks good on the dance floor. It is a core part of male banter. In pubs, golf clubs and WhatsApp groups up and down the land, a man of a certain age will say something a bit depressing, a bit forlorn, a bit genuinely how he's feeling and his friends will respond, 'Jeez, talk about a midlife crisis.' And that's it. Tension released. Awkward moment over. Excellent for keeping us all going on our respective hamster wheels. Less excellent for addressing the underlying problem. Humour is the best defence. But defence is not healthy.

The midlife crisis is by no means an exclusively male experience – anyone is capable of being miserable in their forties – but men are, at least statistically, more likely to be seriously afflicted.

I will explore why this is the case in later chapters, but for now let's just make one ill-advised, gender-based sweeping generalisation. Men are hardwired to suppress their emotions. We wear our emotional illiteracy with pride. We joke about serious issues, we ignore warning signs, we soldier on. This makes it harder for us to admit – to our friends, to our families and, most importantly, most reluctantly, to ourselves – that we're *not* joking and we're *not* okay. That we need help. That we are really struggling.

I. Am. Struggling.

That's hard to say. It suggests fallibility, and fallibility is not something men are conditioned to show. It also suggests predictability. You are a man of a certain age. *Of course* you're struggling. It's right there in the subtitle of the first proper book on the subject: *Predictable Crises of Adult Life*. We don't want to show fallibility and we don't want to be predictable. So we are left with a choice. Either we accept that we have become the midlife cliché, grin and bear the accompanying ridicule and ask for help or we ignore the problem and just carry on. Option B is far more popular than Option A.

Unfortunately, the lives of this particular generation of midlifers have coincided with two unhelpful phenomena that make just carrying on a lot more difficult. First, the working day has become longer and more intense. According to a recent government-funded study, a third of employees say they have to work at very high speeds 'all' or 'almost all' the time. The number of workers breaking the official forty-eight-hour-week limit continues to rise, and those who clock up a gruelling fifty-five-hour week are 40 per cent more likely to have a heart attack.*

Second, the proliferation of mobile technology has blurred the line between working and not working. The smartphone should have made life easier. In reality, it means employees are never more than a four-digit passcode, a thumbprint or a face scan away from work. When the free Wi-Fi service was upgraded on trains running from Aylesbury to London a couple of years ago, academics took the opportunity to study changing passenger behaviour. Their findings were presented at the Royal Geographical Society, very much in the style of a deep-sea explorer bringing news of a new and disturbing type of fish. Sixty per cent

---

* The recent government-funded study is not so recent as to take into account the small matter of a global pandemic. We don't need to have another Zoom meeting to conclude that most employees have not found 2020 any less stressful.

of the passengers were using the faster Wi-Fi to 'catch up' on work emails. 'It's dead time in a way,' explained one of the five thousand – mainly enthusiastic – respondents. 'So what it allows me to do is finish stuff and not work in the evenings.' To which the man with the clipboard should have enquired: 'What about reading a book? What about having some time with your own thoughts? What about just doing nothing? And while we're at it, young man, have you considered the implications of turning dead time into work time? Where will this efficiency end?' Rather than making a case for the elimination of Wi-Fi on trains, the academics argued that the commute should be counted as part of the working day.

But we also have Wi-Fi at home. Indeed, most of us have at least four whole Gs – whatever they are – wherever we are. Think of your phone not as a tool of convenience but as a culvert through which your office stresses can leach into the rest of your life.

'I never stopped to consider that I would effectively be an absentee dad,' says another midlife City worker who commutes from the nether regions of Sussex. 'The priorities were, I suppose, old fashioned: to have my partner at home with the children and to have me providing. Now I think we should have spent more time working out what would have made us all happier.' This is a common theme: the realisation that more planning and less going with the traditional flow would have been a good idea.

'I hate my job. And I couldn't give a toss if I'm a success or not. But it's too late to change now,' says a forty-four-year-old pharmaceutical executive with a familiar sense of abject resignation. 'I've just renegotiated our mortgage. Back to twenty-five years for the third time. The building society kindly pointed out that I'll be sixty-nine when it finishes, but I assured them I'd still be working. I wasn't lying. I think I'll always be working.'

The twenty-fourth person I interview is the first to say that having children has made him more ambitious, rather than less. He works in the visual-effects industry and is as happy as he's ever been in his job. He finds it stimulating, mentally rewarding and, *sui generis*, worth getting up for in the morning. He even claims that he would still go to work if money were no issue – like one of those infuriating lottery winners who announce to the cameras, glass of champagne in one hand, phone-number cheque in the other, that they won't be giving up the day job. He is a sparkling outlier, bucking the fortysomething inertia-and-depression trend. Could he have all the answers? If I ask the right questions, perhaps we could wrap up this whole book before the end of this Introduction.

Well, I do my best. But after twenty minutes of gentle poking and less gentle prodding, it becomes clear that his rosy outlook is rather fragile. 'In my twenties, I was fuelled by a curiosity of the new,' he explains. 'Pretty much any career risk was worth taking. But now there is enormous pressure on me as the provider to keep the ship afloat.' This growing aversion to risk is already having a knock-on effect on his work–life balance. The night before our interview, his wife cooked 'a proper dinner'. He had promised to leave work by six, but stepped gingerly through the front door at nine. The previous week, having assured her he would leave the office at eight, he had crept in at two in the morning. Over the summer, he was forced to abandon his young family midway through their seaside holiday due to a work crisis in Brussels. He has managed to attend only one parents' evening since his kids started school. 'I think more damaging than all of this is the brain space that work takes up in the evenings and weekends when I should be focused on the family. You don't just turn the tap off when you leave work. Most of the time I'm utterly exhausted and stressed, and I'm not home early enough on weekdays to achieve what you'd call a good balance.'

The single-income dads I interview invariably describe their setups as 'important', 'a sacrifice' and/or 'a partnership'. 'With two incomes, we could have a bigger house or more holidays,' says one, 'but we didn't want our children raised by a nanny.'

'My wife compromised on her career to bring up our daughters,' says another. 'She sacrificed her work. I sacrificed time with the family, which I'll never get back. We wouldn't have done it any other way. Or rather, we didn't spend enough time thinking if there was another way to do it.'

Those families in which both parents work make different sorts of sacrifices. 'We live in a small flat in London,' says one dad. 'That was the only way we could both continue our careers and get back in reasonable time for the children. We couldn't both work and both have a long commute.'

Others speak of their guilt. 'Neither of us gave up our career,' explains a lawyer in a two-lawyer family. 'We both sometimes wish we had been more present when the children were younger. We sacrificed time with them so we could give them a good life. That was probably a mistake, but there's no point in worrying about it now.'

Regardless of the set-up, the pros, the cons, the different ways of muddling through, the thread that runs through all of these lives is acceptance. Frequently, though, that thread unravels into total resignation. Aspirations have been abandoned, responsibility has superseded ambition and happiness has become an unaffordable luxury. The prevailing belief, entrenched over the decades, is that this is just part of life. It is the all-too-predictable midlife slump. Just be glad it's not the full-on implosion. Hunker down for the next five or ten years, and you'll be okay.

This resignation is at the heart of all those self-help books and videos. It's going to happen, so why not turn your midlife crisis into 'a positive experience'? If you feel stuck, here's how to unstick. Anything is possible. You are only limited by your imagination. Great things never come from comfort zones. Push yourself because no one else is going to do it for you. If you weren't happy yesterday, try something different today. *Et cetera, ad infinitum.* Aaaargghh!

It is not that simple. How could it be?

One of the more recent anxieties keeping me awake in the small hours is that readers will come to this book hoping for a quick fix. That's not your fault. It's mine. After all, just look at that subtitle. *Why Men Are Unhappy and What We Can Do About It* implies some sort of remedy, doesn't it? Maybe a simple one will emerge. Or maybe, I fret under the duvet, it will be far more complicated than that and you'll be left just as grumpy as I am every time I click, desperately, on 'Five ways to improve your life ... today.'

We prefer order to chaos, and we like our problems to have solutions. On this the wellness industry, solutions-orientated to the core, is built. Confess your midlife troubles to a wellness practitioner and, depending on their speciality, they'll advise meditation, yoga, Pilates, reiki, Valerian root, aromatherapy, cryotherapy, crystals, cannabidiol, psilocybin or straight-up past-life regression. Or a sound bath. Or an emotional-support kangaroo. Or otonamaki.* I've tried most of these approaches – not otonamaki – and they are, to varying degrees, okay. Some help more than others. None was a game-changer. Although the soundbath was great.

So, barring some great mid-book epiphany in which it turns out that the unrelenting grind of midlife experience can be cured with six sessions of hydrotherapy and a rectal steam – fingers crossed – it seems like we're all missing the point. Or, more specifically, it seems like we're treating the symptoms rather than trying to find a cure (or, better still, a vaccine). If, as appears to be the case, millions of men are doing everything 'right' and their reward is profound unhappiness, then maybe doing everything 'right' is ... wrong. Could there be a healthier definition of 'success'? Could there be a better way to be a man?

Two hurdles stand in the way of answering these questions. First, and with good reason, it is unfashionable to point out that men are struggling. After all, we have stacked

---

* Surely you've paid someone to swaddle you in cotton and leave you in the foetal position for half an hour?

the cards in our favour ever since we were hunting woolly mammoths. Second, when we do admit we're struggling, we are immediately inundated with ways to fix it and left with no time to understand the underlying issues. It's the equivalent of a doctor dishing out painkillers.

In this book, I will focus – unfashionably – on men. I think we have reached the point where it's worth exploring and stress-testing the male experience. Painkillers will be dished out only *in extremis*. We're going to take a more holistic look at what's going on, man. What is it about the structures of society and the conditioning of men that leads to the existential angst of midlife? Is it treatable? Is it curable? Can we develop – *cough* – herd immunity?

Over the next nine chapters, I will examine what makes the modern man. I'll start at the very beginning – with school and playground psychology, followed by the perils of early relationships – before exploring each phase of our adult lives, from the roaring twenties through to fatherhood, midlife and the happy ever after. Along the way, I'll question our relationships with our own physical and mental health and our attitudes to success and money. I'll explain why we prioritise the wrong things over the right things; why we prefer to soldier on rather than stop and sort things out.

When I started researching this book, I felt that Gail Sheehy was right to stick the word 'predictable' in front of her 'life crises'. Now, I'm not so sure. In the course of speaking to other men and many thoughtful experts, I started to experience a strange, unfamiliar emotion – I think you might call it hope.

As I write, my eldest son, Freddie, is digesting his year nine report. If he concentrates, he has 'great potential', it says. He is fourteen and already anxious. So, can we predict a life crisis for him in three decades' time? My middle son, Felix, is awaiting his eleven-plus results. What about him? The youngest, Eli, is making mud cakes in the garden. So at least he's still all to play for.

As for me – and the rest of us midlifers – it's tempting to say it's far too late. We're stuck and – barring a Damascene yoga stretch – that's it. But over the course of this project – spoiler alert – my outlook has changed. I may not be the happiest man in Britain (I'll introduce you to him later – you're not ready yet), but at least I'm no longer miserable. Not all the time, anyway. Hopefully, by the end of this book, you might feel that way too. We may as well start optimistic, right?

CHAPTER ONE

Boys and school

When I was six, Daniel Higson – a boy as wide as he was tall – took a cartoon run-up from a grass bank and punted my *Star Wars* lunchbox across the playground. As my absolutely gleeful primary school colleagues and I watched my Wotsits and Um Bungo sail through the air, I thought, 'So this is my life. I work hard, I keep a low profile, I invite everyone to my birthday party ... and my lunch still gets vaporised.' I wanted to cry but prison rules applied. I would have to save my tears for the walk home.

As the laughter turned to chanting and I tried to herd the remnants of my lunch back into the splintered container, no one helped. Friends melted into the crowd. You couldn't really blame them – they didn't want to be next. It was every boy for himself. Dog eat dog. Friend let down friend. A nice lesson to learn when you're still on most of your milk teeth. For the next five interminable years, I ate my lunch like a meerkat.

Then I went to the local grammar school. Hurrah for me. All boys. All wildly misunderstood testosterone and pimples. It was like that episode of *Planet Earth* when a group of young, dumb polar bears try to sort out which one is the alpha male. Except, in our episode, the sorting out was confined to break time, geography (no discipline) and the changing rooms after Wednesday PE. At all other times, the polar bears had to sit in a classroom without talking, fidgeting or exhibiting any signs of youthful exuberance. Failure to comply was rewarded with lines on a blackboard. Or a flying board rubber. Or detention.

School is where all this starts. It's where you learn what is and isn't acceptable for a man. Emotions are contained. Exuberance is dampened. Expectations are defined. School is the first step down a very clearly marked path that leads directly to the stress and unhappiness of midlife. And we accept this. It's routine. It's a 'good thing', even though any man of a certain age – or any age – can reel off countless horror stories about his school days. The time he was wedgied in the loos. The time he was sucker-punched outside the fifth-form disco. The time the whole assembly sang 'Moley, Moley, Moley' instead of 'Holy, Holy, Holy' because he had a mole on his cheek that he had previously thought unnoteworthy but, it turned out, made him the school's Singing Detective. Those are just mine, dug up from the shallow grave in which I have tried to bury them. I'm sure every other middle-aged man has his own.

Certainly all of my interviewees recall traumatic dealings with the school bully, whereas none admits to being the bully himself. Maybe a few are hiding the truth, but it's more likely that even the bullies felt bullied at school. So I suppose I should feel sorry for Daniel Bloody Higson.

'I remember school as just a years-long exercise in trying not to stick out,' confides a man who is now, not entirely coincidentally, a university ethics lecturer. 'If you were too much of a know-it-all in class, you attracted attention from your peers. If you showed the requisite amount of disdain for learning to avoid that attention, the teachers made your life a misery.'

'I just remember being unbelievably, endlessly, interminably bored,' says another middle-aged interviewee. 'History lessons were death. We had these sheets with a paragraph of text and then a paragraph of lines. The teacher told us what to write on the lines. Word for word. For weeks, months and years. I used to look out of the window from our prefab classroom and wish I was a bee.'

Boredom is the most common memory. Fear of exclusion from the pack comes a close second. Fear of failure is also right up there. 'I failed the eleven-plus and that pretty much scarred me for life,' says a man who now runs a successful marketing agency. 'I always tell people it was the best thing that ever happened to me, that it spurred me on to make a go of life, but that's very much a hindsight thing. At the time, I felt worthless. No matter how much everyone said it didn't matter, it was just an arbitrary test, I still struggled with my own self-worth. I was socially awkward, withdrawn even, all through secondary school and, when I did well in my exams, I felt like I didn't deserve it. Even now, running my own company, I feel like an impostor. I feel like my team must be smarter than me.'

Then there's the straight-A student who could never do enough to please his parents. 'I was helicopter-parented before helicopter-parenting was a thing,' he says. 'My father marked my teachers' marks. When kids made fun of me for being a swot, I was told that they were only jealous. I don't know what they had to be jealous about because I spent my adolescence learning dates in history and conjugations in German. They spent theirs meeting girls. I went to a great university, developed a considerable drug habit, wrecked all my relationships and only grew up in my thirties. They all did much better. I behaved like an adult at school and a child for the rest of my life. I try not to think about that too much – it's upsetting.'

Overall, the interviewees have few positive memories of their schooling. Misery was the default setting, peppered with fleeting happier moments, such as 'We had one teacher who hated the curriculum as much as we did, so we loved her,' and 'The school shut for a fortnight when the boiler burst; we all went tobogganing.' The phrase 'I love school' was simply not part of the lexicon for the vast majority of schoolboys in the eighties.

This has a lot to do with the fundamentals of the education system. Until the age of four, we were free to cycle around the block in our dungarees and make mud cakes and catapults and worm soup. Then, after one last summer of freedom, we were given a bowl cut, dressed in neatly ironed uniforms and asked to smile for the camera. Like we'd accidentally joined the army. 'Your first day of school,' our parents told us. 'Aren't you a big boy now? We're so proud.' Because school was a good thing.

Twelve to fourteen years later, we came out the other end. The effect those years had on us was measured not by anything wishy-washy like happiness or empathy or sociability, but by grades on a piece of paper. If those grades were good, everything was fine. If they weren't, everything was a disaster. You were either a success or a failure. You were good or bad. You were ready for the binary judgementalism of adult life. Brutal.

Before the 1800s, education was the preserve of the wealthy. Then the Victorians arrived with their big plans. Full of righteous, evangelical, imperial zeal, they looked at the huddled masses, wrinkled their noses and decided enough was enough. First, there would be Sunday school. Let's see if we can teach these gin-swigging urchins some moral fibre. Then there would be more extensive – if sporadic – schooling, courtesy of a network of church societies. Finally, with the passing of several landmark acts towards the end of the nineteenth century, there would be education for all. Hurrah for the benevolent Victorians.

Now, I'm not going to argue that universal education is a bad thing, no matter how much I hated – absolutely hated – double maths and have never, not once, needed trigonometry to make it through the day. If the choice is between tailored education for the wealthy elite or one-size-fits-all education for everyone, then, clearly, we have to

opt for the latter. Education is freedom even when it feels
like it definitely is not. But I *am* going to argue that those
Victorians' motives were deeply suspect. Their focus wasn't
on some belated English Enlightenment. They weren't
introducing literacy programmes for the joy of reading.
And they certainly weren't trying to spread resources more
evenly or increase social mobility. If anything, the early
school system was specifically designed to enhance control and subjugation. It was an industrial response in an
industrial age, but its flaws are still damaging children in
post-industrial Britain.

You can trace the curriculum my generation endured
right back to those first church-funded schools of the
mid-nineteenth century. The powers that be decided what
should be prioritised on the syllabus – good behaviour,
good behaviour, Bible studies and good behaviour. As a
result, the Victorian classroom was a grim, joyless place.
The decor was austerity-chic. The walls were bare, except
for snippets of instructive scripture. The windows were
positioned above head height to avoid distracting views of
flora or fauna. (The Victorians' relationship with nature
was almost as conflicted as their relationship with sex.)
Learning was by rote. Those who fell behind were humili-
ated with the dunce's cap.

A century later, as Daniel Higson was taking it upon
himself to dish out his own blunt brand of humiliation,
not much had changed. The style of teaching had become
a little more interactive and, although I was slippered in my
first year of secondary school for not falling asleep quickly
enough on a field trip to Devon, corporal punishment was

on the way out.* But the structure and purpose of mass education had hardly changed at all. School was still a means to instil good behaviour through tight discipline. We still sat in a stifling class of thirty, in a room with windows above head height, wondering if the batteries in the wall clock had died of boredom.

In addition, like generations before us, we had to cope with a properly regulated sense of foreboding. Or, as the Department for Education calls it, examination. Imagine a group of bewigged nineteenth-century legislators sitting in a Westminster committee room, discussing the nation's youth. The conversation would have been laden with all sorts of humanitarian points about raising standards, helping the poor and eliminating the loopholes that tyrannical mill owners were exploiting to keep Britain's underage workforce on the production line. Very little of it would have involved any consideration for the children themselves.

'I know,' says Bewigged Chap A. 'Let's introduce examinations.'

'Capital idea,' says Bewigged Chap B. 'And let's link funding to the results. That way, we'll guarantee higher

---

* After much conjecture, the cane was finally banned in state schools in 1986 and independent schools in 1999. Not everyone thought this was progress: a group of forty religious schools appealed against the legislation in the European Court of Human Rights. Phil Williamson, headmaster of the Christian Fellowship School in Edge Hill, Liverpool, said, 'It is not back to a Dickensian age of six of the best. We are not seeking that. What we are seeking is reasonable, moderate and loving discipline. It has a beneficial effect on some children.' The appeal was rejected. Williamson's pupils would just have to manage without his loving discipline.

standards throughout this great land and all of Her Majesty's empire.'

Behold the Revised Code of Minutes and Regulations of the Committee of the Privy Council on Education, 1862. It specified that Parliament's annual grant for public education would be distributed on the basis of results. Each pupil would have to sit an examination in reading, writing and 'rithmetic. If they passed, the school would receive some money. Within a year of the Revised Code's introduction, most schools were teaching to the test. Standards fell and pressure on the children increased.

It would have been sensible to drop exams there and then, and switch to a more holistic approach to learning. Obviously that didn't happen. I sat my A-levels twenty-seven years ago, but I still have a recurring nightmare about one of them. I've done all the revision for my history exam. I've learnt all the dates like an upwardly mobile Victorian urchin. There is nothing I don't know, superficially, about Henry VIII's Reformation and the origins of the First World War (incidentally, two perfect examples of miserable men making unwise choices on the basis of fear and insecurity). But when I arrive in the examination hall I realise I don't have a pen. The invigilator, who happens to be the mother of my first girlfriend, hands me a ballpoint that works inter-mittently, at best, but I'm far too nervous to ask for another, given how that relationship ended.

'Turn over your papers. The time starts now.'

That's a horrible memory in itself, isn't it? So full of dread anticipation. What if Henry VIII doesn't come up? What if the questions are written in Swahili? But in this particularly sneaky nightmare, it's all fine. It's what I've studied. So, for the next two dream hours, I simply resit my A-level. Then my first girlfriend's mum says, 'Put your pens down,' and I wake up, exhausted. I would rather have the Swahili nightmare. Or one in which I'm naked at my desk. Either of those would be less cruel than just ploughing through the actual exam over and over and over again.

Astonishingly, our reliance on exams and testing has actually increased since I was at school. As well as GCSEs and A-Levels, we have OFSTED reports and bloody SATs. Every school lives or dies by its ranking, so there's more pressure on the pupils to behave, and more pressure on the teachers to teach to the test. The inevitable result is that British children are now among the most tested in the world ... and among the most stressed. It's almost as if those two things could be linked.*

When Freddie, our eldest, apple of my eye, started nursery, he was illiterate, unsure on his feet and unable – or unwilling – to wipe his bum. In other words, he was a year old. At that age, he could spend an entire morning chasing pigeons and leaves around the local park with the joy and determination of either a very drunk man or a person who has

---

* Every year, on results day, Jeremy Clarkson tweets a variation on 'Don't worry if your results are disappointing. I got a C and two Us and I'm currently on a super-yacht in the Med.' It's a valiant attempt to help those students who feel as if their whole lives have just been tipped into the abyss. But Clarkson's personal success doesn't alter the fact that so much rides on how well students can remember facts within a short amount of time on a certain day. This is obviously devastating for those who can't, but I think it's also damaging for those who can. To understand why, please continue reading.

found true meaning in life. It would have taken at least ten years of daily yoga, meditation and wheatgrass smoothies for an adult to attain his ability to live in the present.

'Look, Daddy, a leaf ... Look, Daddy, a pigeon ... Look, Daddy, a leaf.'

But then off he went to nursery in an antiseptic prefab classroom just down the road from us. He only did two days a week, but those days felt like an eternity for us, so Christ knows what they must have been like for him. He didn't know what was going on. Where were the leaves? Where were the pigeons? Where were the leaves? As we said goodbye at drop-off, he gave us the mournful look of a dog that is on its way to the vet's. It just knows something bad is going to happen, doesn't it?

As a parent, you convince yourself it will all be fine, even though the government has thirty-seven pages of very prescriptive guidelines for preschool teaching but not one that says, 'Remember, they're just toddlers ... they just want to have fun. Chill out.' Nurseries, you remind yourself, focus on play-based learning these days, which is at least half right. It should be fun and there aren't any exams because that really would be ridiculous. Except, to a degree, there are. Each Friday, Freddie would come home not only with that lingering look of a betrayed dog but also clutching a detailed log – including photographic evidence – of his activities that week. Alongside each entry, there would be a note about his progress.

Not long after he turned four, Freddie was off to school. Bigger classroom. More tables and chairs. The same old high windows to keep out nature. Sure, there were some colourful posters on the wall, and it wasn't like he was forced to learn Latin by rote and wear a dunce's cap if he fluffed his *eram*, *eras*, *erat*. But still, there were phonics and maths and stickers if he was good and a soft toy if he was very good.

The soft toy wasn't for keeps. Oh no. It would come home for just a night – a special guest for a special boy – carrying the germs of every previous goody two-shoes, and Freddie, still only four, would have to write a fun account of its brief time with us. If several days passed without a visit from the sweaty, sticky corona-monkey, Freddie would start to worry. He was obviously not good enough. Maybe he was even bad? That bloody monkey – or rather its absence – was basically a twenty-first-century dunce's cap. And we weren't in the clear even when it did visit, because Freddie would worry that we weren't doing anything sufficiently fun to report. It didn't help that other parents were already embroiled in an arms race.

'We took Monkey to McDonald's.'

'Well, we took Monkey to Wagamama.'

'Well, we took Monkey to the English National Opera. He loved *The Marriage of Figaro*.'

Competition. Success. The threat of failure. Anxiety about not being as 'good' as everyone else. Critical life lessons that will make Freddie miserable by the time he's my age.

Helen Davenport, a senior lecturer at Manchester Metropolitan University, spent ten years as a primary school teacher before retraining as an expert in forest schools and a teacher of teachers. She has a three-year-old son called Jack and is concerned about the testing culture in our education system.

'The nursery sent us a video of Jack as part of their developmental record,' she tells me. 'He was playing the bongos and all the other children were having a tribal dance. He was lost in that moment with those drums and it was just awesome.' The accompanying analysis – there's *always* some sort of analysis – read, 'Jack is achieving his British values.'

The nursery staff had evidently looked down a long list of developmental criteria. In the absence of 'playing bongos', they'd plumped for 'achieving British values'.

'I suppose he wasn't pissing anyone off,' Davenport says, with a frustrated laugh. 'He was being a good citizen.'

She describes all this in terms of ever-decreasing circles: 'The testing culture just gets pushed down and down. You have SATs in year six and year two. And although the foundation stage is supposed to be play-based, you have phonics tests in year one. So now preschools are trying to gear up for that. I can walk into a nursery and they're doing stuff I wouldn't want to introduce until at least year one.'

There is, she says, a lot of fear in schools: 'They're very observed and scrutinised in terms of accountability and reputation and parents wanting certain things. At the heart of it are a lot of awfully good teachers trying to create some wriggle room, some freedom around the curriculum.'

Freedom? Wriggle room? Why are these particularly important for boys? As I said in the Introduction, it's dangerous – potentially career suicide – to make sweeping generalisations based on gender, but several studies in Britain, the United States and Scandinavia have found one key difference between boys and girls at a young age: put simply, girls are better at self-regulation than boys. They are more likely to be able to sit still and complete a task.

'There are boys who just want to be outside. Or, if they want to try writing something, they want to do it *big* ... on a wall or with chalk on the patio,' says Davenport. 'They're not going to want to sit at a desk with their crayons. They have exuberance and spontaneity but that doesn't necessarily fit with what's required of them in the classroom. They have to be "good", whatever that means.'

So, why are girls better at self-regulating? 'We should be curious about this too,' says Davenport. 'What happens to girls' exuberance? Does that get squashed before they even get to preschool?'

That's a depressing thought. Those who do best in a classroom setting are those who've already had their exuberance squashed. They are rewarded for fitting in, given gold stars and soft toys to take home, while those who aren't ready are not. According to Davenport, this dichotomy can have a damaging long-term impact: 'If, for example, you start off with phonics in the first term, these little boys are already getting the feeling that there's something going on here that they can't do. It can have a knock-on effect for their whole education.'

On a Friday afternoon a week before we spoke, Davenport had been in the woods south of Birmingham with a group of nine-year-olds. For one day a week, these kids escape their classroom and attend 'forest school'. Created in Denmark in the 1950s, forest school is now an integral part of the curriculum for the majority of Scandinavian children up to the age of seven. Proponents say that this early-learning environment gives children the time and space to develop social skills, leadership, collaboration and self-esteem. I'm prepared to bet you one shattered Luke Skywalker lunch-box that they are happier as a result. It's a safe bet, because I've checked the statistics and they are.

In the UK, the forest school movement has been steadily growing since its arrival here in the 1990s. In some cases, its introduction has been little more than a marketing exercise – a token session every now and again to allow a school to add 'forest learning' to its prospectus. 'It's very fashionable to say you have a forest school,' says Davenport, 'but to have an impact, it needs to be week on week, so you build trust between the children and adults, and among the children themselves.'

On that particular Friday afternoon in the woods, some girls made twig crowns and some boys made a mudslide. Unlike that very Victorian approach that still persists today – that learning should take place in a controlled environment, free from all distractions – the forest school ethos advocates reconnecting pupils with nature. It also gives them freedom. They can decide what they want to do. They are trusted to plan and lead their own activities. There is no one with a clipboard and a set of guidelines.

One boy spent the entire four hours lopping willow until he had amassed a large pile of uniform twigs. 'I don't know why he was doing that, but it was what he needed to do,' says Davenport. Another boy set himself a classic caveman challenge: try to light a fire with a spark. Inevitably, he struggled, but the rest of the group gathered around him, offering encouragement. Then, after almost an hour, the twigs finally started to smoulder. He make fire! His colleagues cheered. 'It's difficult to replicate that in a classroom,' says Davenport. 'In that confined space, you're quickly knocked down. You are identified as being good or bad at something, and that's hard to change once it has been established.'

So what should we do? Should we start formal education later (as they do in Norway, Germany and most other European countries)? Yes, of course we should. The government's argument that 'earlier is better' is not supported by any meaningful evidence. On the contrary, the consequences of starting literacy and numeracy too young can be damaging. Thirteen years ago, this was the key theme of an international conference on foundation-stage learning at the University of Oxford. Lillian Katz, Professor of Education at the University of Illinois, warned the audience that the British model could put children off reading for life: 'The evidence we have so far is that if you start formal teaching of reading very early, the children do well in tests, but when you follow them up to the age of eleven or twelve, they don't do better than those who have had a more informal approach,' she said, before stressing that early formal instruction is particularly counterproductive for half of the pupils. 'Boys are expected to be active and assertive, but during formal instruction they are being passive, not active. In most cultures, girls learn to put up with passivity earlier and better than boys.'

Certainly, those of us who passed through the system in the eighties would have benefited from more time running around, mucking about, not thinking about maths. It's surely not ideal that boredom and fear are the defining memories of our schooling at that time.

Should we stop testing everything and anything that moves? Yes, of course we should. Ranking pupils throughout their education instils a sense of competition rather than cooperation. It teaches us that there are successful people and unsuccessful people from a worryingly formative age. It fails to take into account different temperaments, different ways of learning and different types of intelligence.

And should every child spend at least one day a week in a forest? Yes, of course they should. In the course of a couple of generations, children's 'radius of activity' – the area around the home where they are allowed to roam unsupervised – has declined by 90 per cent. In the 1970s, 80 per cent of seven- and eight-year-olds walked to school, many on their own or with friends. By 2000, this was down to just 10 per cent. Today, it is closer to zero. When it comes to nature and trust, we are even worse than the Victorians. Rewilding school is absolutely essential.

At the heart of all of this, we need to rethink how we motivate children. Teachers are under intense pressure to get their pupils to pass tests. They may be brave enough to take the occasional detour from the curriculum and sneak in a bit of *Dead Poets Society*, but they still need to ensure compliance among their charges. The easiest way to do this is with carrots and sticks. But the sticks were banned back in 1986, so now it's mainly carrots ... and the withholding of carrots.

This is behavioural manipulation – embedded in our culture just as it was embedded in those early Victorian schools. We are conditioned from an early age to conform. And the more we conform, the more treats we will receive, just like Pavlov's poor salivating dogs. We are taught out of all meaningful proportion to find motivation in external factors – gold stars in primary school, good grades in secondary school, an impressive job title in our forties.* We rarely stop to ask whether these rewards really matter. We just keep working to the tests.

To suggest that grades are unimportant and good behaviour is secondary to an enquiring, engaged mind is bordering on anarchy. The system does not allow this kind of hippy nonsense. It is much easier to ignore our misgivings and continue to tick the boxes. At least until the midlife crisis hits.

I was twelve when I had the first bout of the insomnia that has plagued me ever since. It began suddenly – and unexpectedly – on a Tuesday night. My alarm hadn't gone off that morning, so I started my paper round late. It was raining and the newspapers became soaked. A middle-aged, red-faced man on Vine Court Road (posh) opened his door before I managed to squeeze every section of his bloated *Daily Telegraph* through his miserly letter box. He picked up the shreds that had made it through, looked at

---

* Just the word 'impressive' should set alarm bells ringing. Impressive grades. Impressive car. Impressive collection of designer suits. Who are we trying to impress, and why?

them, looked at me, and unleashed a tidal wave of abuse. If iPhones had been invented and I'd managed to film his tirade, it definitely would have gone viral. I was rooted to the spot for so long that I missed the bus and the start of school, which led to another telling off. I looked out of the window in physics. I was told off. I struggled to stay awake in French. I was told off. On the bus home, I felt rising panic. I was shattered and knew I would never get all my homework done.

I didn't get all my homework done, so I set the alarm for half an hour earlier than usual before collapsing into bed. *Ping.* Wide awake. Mind racing. Homework, paper rounds, angry *Telegraph* readers, homework. Eleven o'clock came and went. So did twelve. I put the radio on. I was fully alert for the half-twelve shipping forecast and a whole programme about Brazilian farming. And another about aerosols. About an hour after I finally fell asleep, the alarm went off. Snooze. Alarm. Snooze. Alarm. Late. Angry *Telegraph* reader. Pay attention, Rudd. Wake up, Rudd. Home. Exhausted. Bed. Wide awake. And repeat.

Eventually, Mum took me to the GP. He was sympathetic – like a bearded, 1980s version of Rangan Chatterjee – and explained that my problem required a holistic solution. This turned out to be a relaxation tape on which a man with a creepy voice trotted out platitudes like 'There is nothing to fear,' 'Just breathe deeply and relax,' and 'When you fall asleep, I am going to sneak into your bedroom and take you away.' It was months before I finally had a decent night's sleep.

According to NHS data, hospital appointments in

England for children under fourteen with sleep disorders tripled between 2007 and 2017. Screen overuse, poor diet, lack of exercise and irregular evening routines are all factors. But the root cause of insomnia is stress. And the root cause of stress is fear of failure.

Here I am, in middle age, talking to lots of other middle-aged men about unhappiness. What can we do about it? How can we change? Is there a better way? I've only just started to connect the dots. Our conditioning to climb the ladder, settle down, conform and behave began early. The loss of childhood to the restrictive, rule-based institution of school was a shock we have never fully addressed.

I was thinking about this during a typical conversation with another father the other day. He was worrying about the lack of homework his eldest son was receiving. GCSEs were only three years away, he said. Other schools were pushing their pupils much harder, he claimed. Maybe he should get a tutor.

Just one pint earlier, we had been talking about ourselves rather than our children. He had won a scholarship to a private school, he said. He hated almost every minute of it, but did well enough. He passed the requisite exams and then spent most of his twenties being fast-streamed up various corporate ladders. His midlife rewards are a big office, a dawn wake-up call, early-onset baldness and, he eventually admitted, a constant fear of losing it all – regardless of the fact that 'it all' is a stressful, exhausting life he clearly loathes. He has taken the pressure to succeed from school and stretched it all the way into his miserable forties. And yet, twenty sentences later, he was contemplating getting his son a tutor.

'Don't you worry that your kids will end up like you?' I asked, rather meanly.

'Yes,' he replied, narrowing his eyes. 'But what's the alternative? That I let them fail?'

I launched into a speech about other paths – alternatives to the simple binary of success and failure. He listened politely, shrugged and said he wasn't prepared to risk his kids' futures on my particular brand of midlife crisis. His scepticism was understandable. I find it easier to take the high ground with other men, rather than myself, and with other dads' children, rather than my own. I tell myself that my children's happiness and wellbeing are far more important than their exam results. But I don't have the guts to follow through with that line of thinking. What distresses me most is that my boys are already beginning to exhibit signs of stress. Freddie, at fourteen, is already worrying about his bloody GCSEs. He has one particular report on his mind: he needs to focus, say his teachers, or his grades will suffer. I tell him grades aren't the be all and end all. He doesn't believe me. Why would he?

We put our children in an entirely unsuitable environment, demand conformity and grade them on the basis of that conformity. That's not a healthy way to raise boys ... or girls. It's not a healthy way to live ... full stop.

CHAPTER TWO

Boys and girls

The first time I had sex, it was just like the movies: candle wax, self-raising flour and everything. That's all we need to say about that, so let's move on.

John's account of his first time is typical of how most men address the subject, in that he begins with some mild bragging, followed by a dash of self-deprecating humour.* He only drops the act when I explain that I'm trying to do some serious research and please could he be completely honest.

'I was fourteen,' he begins. 'Pretty young.' That's the bragging. 'It lasted about four seconds. I don't remember much about it, but I'm sure she was very satisfied.' That's the humour. Then, the honesty: 'When it happened, the overwhelming emotion was relief,' he admits. 'As in

---

* *All* interviewees' names in this chapter have been changed ... obviously.

"Thank God that's out of the way." We'd been together for a few weeks and she was a bit older than me. I definitely wasn't ready to have sex, but there was just this pressure. Not from her and not really from everyone else. Not directly anyway. But it was all anyone talked about – girls and what base someone had got to and how a guy in the year above had slept with half of the netball team. Everyone else seemed to be doing everything and then there was me, taking my girlfriend to the cinema once a week and having an innocent kiss on her doorstep afterwards. It was … embarrassing.

'Of course, I subsequently found out that all my mates were exaggerating. Most of them were lying outright. We were all virgins pretending to be sex maniacs. It seems ridiculous now, but at the time I felt like I was walking around with a big "V" tattooed on my forehead. And she felt pressure, too. Her friends were all talking up their sexual experience and it made her feel like a baby.

'So we did it. We did it for all the wrong reasons and, of course, it wasn't great. We carried on going out for almost a year, but we didn't have sex again. It was something that we both felt we had to get out the way. It wasn't that magical experience you see in the movies. It took four more years before I had sex again and by then I was ready. But I still wish I'd been a bit braver and had the confidence to wait.'

Education – the pressure cooker of exam-obsessed, classroom-based learning – sends boys into adult life with a skewed definition of success. In this chapter, I want to look at the other foundations of manhood. On the face of it, they are all about freedom – sexual freedom ('I've lost my virginity!'), financial freedom ('I've found a job!') and logistical freedom ('I've passed my driving test!') – so this should be relatively easy. Young men are finally in the driving seat. We know what we have to do and no one is trying to stop us. Establishing ourselves as proper, grown-up men is not only expected and encouraged but facilitated. 'You're a man now,' our parents and teachers say as they push us into the world that is suddenly our oyster.

It doesn't feel like that at the time. All of those newfound freedoms come with rules and conditions. The ritualised process of becoming a man is confined within a narrow set of parameters. Get it wrong and you risk humiliation. Deviate and you won't succeed. And, as our Pavlovian school experiences have taught us, success is everything. As we try to explain why so many middle-aged men end up miserable, here we find some more seeds of the problem.

When I ask midlifers like John to think back to their first sexual experience, all of their accounts have two things in common. First, the event itself was hugely underwhelming/ awkward/embarrassing; and, second, it was more of a relief than a delight when it finally happened. John is actually something of an outlier because he was just fourteen and understandably unready. Most of the others were older ... but still not ready.

According to the most recent National Survey of Sexual Attitudes and Lifestyles poll, 40 per cent of young women and 26 per cent of young men feel that their first sexual experience happened at the wrong time. Maybe times have changed. Or maybe many of the young men who answer sex surveys aren't always entirely honest. Fortunately, the same survey had some cunning ways to glean a more accurate picture of readiness. Was the respondent in a position to make an informed decision about having sex for the first time? Were they sober? Were they acting under peer pressure? The answers to these questions suggest that almost half of young women and 40 per cent of young men were not ready to lose their virginity.

In our conversations, every single interviewee eventually admitted that he had either lied about his sexual experience or managed to avoid discussing it altogether with his first partner. Andrew finally got his chance when he was nineteen. 'Thank God I did,' he says. 'I was at the point where I was considering taking my vows. I had stopped thinking rationally about it. I just assumed that every girl I met could tell immediately that I was some kind of weird, full-grown virgin. I was only nineteen, but that's about ninety in virgin years.'

Such were the years of increasing panic – and weeks of nervous anticipation when he started going out with a slightly older woman – that when the moment finally came, so did he. It was all over before he got his boxers off. 'It was easily one of the most embarrassing moments of my life,' he says, reddening noticeably at the memory. 'She had come down to stay with me at my university and when the ... umm ... *accident* happened, I leapt out of bed, telling her I needed the toilet, which was obviously, biologically, ridiculous. I ran down the corridor in my underwear, locked myself in a shower cubicle and tried to come up with a plan. I couldn't, not in a million years, tell her what had actually happened, so I did the next most logical thing. I soaked myself with water, head to toe, staggered back to the room and told her some other students had chucked a bucket over the cubicle divide for a laugh. Then I said I was sorry, but the mood had passed.'

Andrew is now in his early forties. He says he has never told anyone this story before, not even his wife, and he won't be telling anyone again. He reports it like we're in a police interview room and he's finally agreed to reveal the location of the bodies. His eyes are fixed on the ceiling. His arms are folded defensively. He is braced for some long-imagined ridicule. 'After an awkward breakfast,' he continues, 'she left the next morning and finished with me by letter the following week. She wrote that she couldn't be with someone who wasn't interested in her and that I should have just been honest. I wrote back explaining that I was very interested in her and that I *was* being honest. I know I wasn't, but I was at least being honest about the thing she thought I wasn't being honest about. What a mess. Two sexual hang-ups – hers and mine – for the price of one.'

Of course, it would be weird if sex education were so detailed and intensive that we all embarked on our sex lives like total players. But the other extreme – naivety, fear and shame – isn't ideal either. I have fairly sketchy memories of sex education lessons. I think that might be my subconscious trying to protect me. I was thirteen and the education came courtesy of our biology teacher. What I can remember is that we spent several weeks of the autumn term learning about *actual* birds and bees. A whole week was devoted to the life cycle of rabbits. Human reproduction, in all its infinite complexity, was covered in one forty-minute period.

The teacher started big, with a watercolour illustration of a penis on the overhead projector. No one listened to what he said because it wasn't a complete penis. It had been sliced in half lengthways, as if by a Samurai sword. All the exposed pipework was rendered in red and livid pink. Some boys sniggered. Most just went pale and crossed their legs.

Next, we were presented with a watercolour of lady parts. There was nothing on the external stuff. It was all very fallopian. Unfazed, the teacher used his long pointer to show us where the sperm fertilised the egg, then how that egg became ... next slide ... a foetus. Then ... next slide ... a whole child. The message was simple: if you get sperm from slide one to slide two, you end up with slides three and four. But no one knew how any of that actually happened, because the way men and women actually had sexual intercourse was not covered. Here are some genitalia, here are some other genitalia, here's the end result when they get together ... and that's the bell. We left knowing three times more about rabbit sex than we did about human sex. For those of us who had no plans to sleep with rabbits, this was surely the wrong way around. We graduated sex education with only the most rudimentary understanding of the mechanics of reproduction and a strong sense that those mechanics could get you into an awful lot of trouble. What a negative way to start learning about sex, love and relationships. Where were the healthy conversations about what it means to be in a relationship? About how the other person can be so much more than the sum of her fallopian tubes? Or about how the other person might not have fallopian tubes? (If sex ed was rudimentary, same-sex ed was non-existent.) Where were the sessions on empathy, feelings and connection? They were certainly nowhere near a British classroom in the 1980s.

In the mid-nineteenth century, medical textbooks were full of the dangers of 'licentiousness and unrestrained indulgence of the passions'.* Medical professionals designed and then prescribed all manner of devices to prevent masturbation and protect what they called a man's 'vital heat'. Those suitably chastised might take to wearing a copper genital straitjacket, a thong made of impenetrable chainmail or, if they were particularly hard on themselves, a silver-plated ring lined with sharp, inward-facing metal teeth.

Some naughty, revisionist historians have made a valiant attempt to recast the hideous Victorians – who must still shoulder the blame for so much of our society's stiff-upper-lip repression – as 'progressive'. Queen Victoria was a bit of a goer, they insist, judging by her quite fruity (an exaggeration) diaries; sex parties were not uncommon in

---

* From consulting surgeon R. J. Brodie's 1845 book *The Secret Companion: A Medical Work on Onanism or Self-Pollution*, in which he also notes that too much masturbation weakens not only the mind and body but the soul. 'We can easily comprehend how there is so close a connection between the brain and testicles,' he wrote, 'because these two organs secern from the blood the most subtle and exquisite lympha, which is destined to give strength and motion to the parts, and to assist even the functions of the soul. So it is probable, that too great a dissipation of these liquors may destroy the powers of the soul, and body.' He must have been great fun at a party.

the upper echelons of society; and pornographic postcards sold by the bucketload. There is even some evidence that married couples occasionally enjoyed sex, notwithstanding the era's most famous agony aunt advice, courtesy of the wife of the second Baron Hillingdon, to 'lie back and think of England.'

But there is no doubt that the prevailing attitude among the moral leaders of our moustachioed forebears was one of instructional reticence. Sexual urges were ungodly and a man should be judged on his ability to conquer those urges.* That was why the Victorians developed, embraced and thoroughly indulged in competitive sport. From the 1860s, contact sport was compulsory in English public schools, and most of the old boys were in no mood to abandon it after they left: 'Not tonight, dear, I'm playing rugger with the chaps.'

As the historian Richard Evans explained in a recent lecture at Gresham College: 'For men, the Victorian ideal of manliness became a way of controlling the feral forces and base instincts of maleness. The Victorian cult of manliness involved the diversion of these base instincts into disciplined aggression. It's not too fanciful to think of the Victorian invention of modern sports – many if not most of which were pioneered in the public schools of

---

* According to the eminent gynaecologist Dr William Acton, women had no such worries. In his pithy 1857 work *The Functions and Disorders of the Reproductive Organs, in Childhood, Youth, Adult Age, and Advanced Life, Considered in the Physiological, Social, and Moral Relations*, he wrote, 'The majority of women (happily for them) are not very much troubled with sexual feeling of any kind.'

the day – as a form of displacement for sexual urges into physical aggression.'*

Young men were expected to be stoic, strong, rational and unemotional, as evidenced most succinctly in Rudyard Kipling's 'If':

> *If you can keep your head when all about you*
> *Are losing theirs ...*
> *If you can make one heap of all your winnings*
> *And risk it on one turn of pitch-and-toss,*
> *And lose, and start again at your beginnings ...*
> *You'll be a Man, my son!*

God, I hate that poem. I hate the fact that some of its verses still crop up on the Instagram feeds of the most saccharine motivational coaches. I hate its sabre-rattling, imperialist overtones – Kipling in full flow as 'bard of the Empire'.

---

* Incidentally, sex paranoia was also why cornflakes were invented. The Michigan doctor John Harvey Kellogg was born in 1852 to Seventh Day Adventists who, among other things, believed the Second Coming was imminent. He had seventeen siblings and half-siblings, which goes some way to explaining why he and his wife abstained from sex altogether (their children were adopted in order to save themselves from the horrors of copulation). With the compunction of a true zealot, Kellogg devoted his life to helping others resist the temptations of the flesh. First, he wrote anti-copulation books, one of which detailed no fewer than thirty-nine gruesome symptoms of 'self-pollution', including bad posture, stiff joints and a fondness for spicy foods. Then he became the Gillian McKeith of his day, albeit with a focus on genitals rather than poo, advocating healthy eating as the easiest way to curb sexual enthusiasm. Like Gillian, he also developed a line of commercial products. The first of his anti-masturbation inventions was an oatmeal biscuit, which, to its credit, was anything but erotic. The second was a yogurt enema – to be taken half orally and half rectally. The third was Kellogg's Cornflakes. They caught on and nobody ever masturbated again.

Most of all, I hate its dishonesty. Kipling's parents sent him from India to England at the age of five. He left the warm and loving embrace of Bombay and found himself on the dank south coast, where he was subjected to the physical and psychological tortures of an evangelical foster mother. Predictably, he struggled to form attachments later in life and saved his passions not for his marriage but for his militaristic patriotism.*

Kipling aside, our attitudes to sex have waxed and waned over the decades. The 1860s were, in some ways, just as permissive as the 1960s. The 1920s were quite louche. During the Second World War, promiscuity seemed like a very sensible way to cope with the threat of Nazism. Throughout it all, though, we've never quite managed to eradicate our shame. The prudishness established under the auspices of Victorian morality has been passed from one embarrassed generation to the next. Which is annoying because sex, according to a tongue-in-cheeked Philip Larkin, was invented in 1963, the year the Beatles arrived and *Lady Chatterley's Lover* was set free, the year which prompted Larkin to compose 'Annus Mirabilis'. Larkin was much more in touch with his feelings than Kipling, noting of his pre-1963 adolescence, 'a shame that started at sixteen/and spread to everything'.

---

* When his son John's attempts to enlist in the First World War were rejected on medical grounds, Kipling used his connections to get him into the Irish Guards. John was subsequently killed in action at the Battle of Loos in 1915, but Kipling merely railed against Britain's leaders for the army's unpreparedness. Such a stiff-upper-lipped approach to personal grief wasn't healthy then and it isn't healthy now.

Thank God that was all over and we could crack on with the Age of Aquarius.

So why were my classmates and I still looking at watercolour diagrams of Samurai-sworded penises in the 1980s? Why was 'relationships education' only added to the national curriculum in September 2020? The answer is that we're still prudish.

The government is finally taking a more enlightened, holistic approach to sex only out of absolute necessity. Adolescence today is far more complicated than it was a generation ago. Back then, our best hope of finding out what the opposite sex looked like naked was to find a discarded dirty magazine in a hedge. Now, young people have internet pornography in all its violent, angry, misogynistic, pneumatic, derogatory, ten-foot-penised glory to guide their attitude to relationships. And where we had nothing but playground Chinese whispers, they have social media.

As a result, we have to overcome our prudishness. The shame of Larkin's generation, which was still alive and well in the 1980s, sent my generation into adult life with an unhealthy level of insecurity about relationships. It made us camouflage our true feelings with bravado or defensiveness. It was still possible to lose the shame and embarrassment, but only after several years in a proper relationship. Invariably, that cathartic process was guided by a woman. So many of my conversations with middle-aged men start with 'If it wasn't for my wife ...' or 'I was useless until I met ...' And I'm no different. My emotional education was belatedly administered by two long-term girlfriends and then a very patient wife.

How quick we are to leave the emotional labour to women. And if we don't, how easily all of our shame, anxiety and ignorance can develop into toxic masculinity. We always fear what we don't understand.

The concept of the 'male gaze' was first coined by the feminist film critic Laura Mulvey in her 1975 essay 'Visual Pleasure and Narrative Cinema'. Mulvey made the unarguable point that classic Hollywood cinema invariably portrays the female as the object of male desire, with very little agency and a lot of 'to-be-looked-at-ness'. She is there solely for the benefit of the hero ... and the lucky male viewer.

Mulvey was writing about the film industry of the mid-twentieth century, but plenty of critics have pointed out that the male gaze is still alive and well in film, on television, in music and advertising a good eighty years later. *Entourage*, a 2015 (pre-Weinstein) buddy movie in which the men are good-timers and the girls lie on yachts in bikinis, is the perfect – if excruciating – example. The line that encapsulates the whole foundation upon which Hollywood culture is built is delivered by Ari Gold, a studio boss and super-agent: 'That's what stars do,' he says in a self-referential scene designed to make it all seem okay. 'They walk into rooms and fuck girls that civilians want.'

The girls are the object, the stars are the subject, the civilians are the male audience. The assumption is that the male audience is fine with this. Aren't we lucky to have an entire film industry catering to our needs and desires? It doesn't matter that, as a male film and television audience, we have as much – or as little – agency as the female audience sharing our popcorn. We could, of course, do more to register our disdain for the persistent male gaze, but that's asking a lot. The young men who see these movies are still finding their way in the world. They are learning the ropes, looking for cues, trying to live up to whatever society expects of them. It's a difficult time for them before you even get to the rights and wrongs of the way women are portrayed on screen. Surely it's up to the studio bosses and television executives to give them something less damaging?

While we're at it, let's take a minute to examine how *men* are portrayed on screen. According to blockbuster orthodoxy, the Hero gets the girl/bikini-clad sex object because he is, by definition, heroic. He has a fearless approach to life, work and alien invasions, and you could chop wood with his jawline. He can operate cranes, gun turrets and hadron colliders without consulting the manual. He always has the perfect quip and never has dandruff. He can undress both himself and the beautiful girl he met five minutes earlier with a confident smile and a click of his fingers. That's quite a lot to live up to for a callow virgin trying to work out the intricacies of the birds and the bees.

But fear not, callow virgin. There are other role models. There's the Big Shot – a man defined by his professional status with an aggressively charismatic, Teflon approach to Monday mornings, nice suit, flashy car and unquenchable self-assurance in board meetings. There's the Joker – the life but not the soul of the party who uses humour as a mask to shield how he really feels, but that doesn't matter because girls love a funny guy. And finally, most common of all, more common even than the Hero, there's Absolutely Useless Guy – can't wash, can't clean, can't operate a dishwasher, can't drive, can't do it himself, can't hold down a job, can't get off the sofa, can't take obvious clues from his emotionally superior girlfriend/wife/mother, can't express how he really feels (just like all the other male characters on screen). He is utterly, irredeemably feckless.* In the recent rush to cast stronger female leads, Absolutely Useless Guy has become even more prevalent in films, on television and in advertising. Because how better to show that you're a studio boss who has moved with the times than to cast your strong female lead against a weak male one?

In 2018, the Advertising Standards Authority announced a clampdown on gender stereotyping: 'Our review shows that specific forms of gender stereotypes in ads can contribute to harm for adults and children,' Ella Smillie, lead author of the report, told the newspapers at the time. 'Such portrayals can limit how people see themselves, how others see them, and limit the life decisions they take. Tougher standards in the areas we've identified will address harms and ensure that modern society is better represented.' Ads should not, for example, feature a man with his feet up while a woman cleans around him. Nor should they portray a 'person with a physique that does

---

* According to a YouGov analysis, once you remove *Blue Planet* and *BBC News* from the running, the most popular UK television shows of all time are *Only Fools and Horses* (feckless men), *Fawlty Towers* (feckless husband), *The Flintstones* (feckless husband again), *Blackadder* (feckless and fecklesser) and *Mr Bean* (genius).

not match an ideal stereotypically associated with their gender' having a tough time in the romance department as a result. And men who found it hilariously impossible to change nappies would end up on the cutting-room floor, where they belonged.

Six months later, when the stricter regulations came into force, the ASA – displaying an admirably gender-neutral approach to its new censoriousness – immediately banned a Volkswagen ad that showed men doing engineering on a space station while a woman made sandwiches *and* a Philadelphia ad in which a new dad left his baby on a sushi conveyer belt. Because mmm, Philadelphia.

Obviously, both of these adverts belong in the bin, but a Mary Whitehouse approach to gender can take us only so far. What we need is a complete reboot. The traditional view of gender as a see-saw – if one side is strong, the other must be weak – sends a bleak message to young men and women. Characters' attributes – both positive and negative – should be based on who they are, not what gender they are. This has long been a feminist campaigning issue because, of course, women have borne the brunt of gender stereotyping since the beginning of gender stereotyping. But we should also recognise that it cuts both ways. The Absolutely Useless Guy stereotype reinforces the idea that young men can be emotionally stunted and need mothering. And the Six-Pack Guy only makes those young men feel even more inadequate.

In the Amazon, thirteen-year-old boys from the Sateré-Mawé tribe mark their coming of age by wearing gloves

filled with bullet ants – reportedly* the most painful stingers in the insect world – on several ceremonial occasions
over a period of months. On Baffin Island, Inuit teenagers
head off into the Arctic tundra with their fathers to learn
how to hunt. In Kenya and Tanzania, Maasai boys sleep
in the forest before returning to drink a cow's-blood cock-
tails and have their foreskins sliced off. It would be foolish
to suggest we adopt any of these ancient initiation rituals.
Proving you're brave enough not to cry while wearing a
bullet-ant glove is not the sort of manliness that is com-
patible with Western culture. We're already bad enough
at showing our emotions. What is important is that all of
these groups have a way to honour their coming of age.
The community comes together, elders welcome the youths
to adulthood, dads share trade secrets with their sons and,
okay, there might be a bit of circumcision, but there's also
guidance. The arrival of manhood is celebrated.

Is there any equivalent in our own increasingly secular
society? Well, Jewish boys still have the bar mitzvah and
observant Christians still have first communion, but we
heathens are reduced to what we can glean from television,
advertising, pornography and our still-quite-embarrassed
educational system. In short, we have a news blackout on
the process of becoming a man. That was certainly how it
was in the eighties. Notwithstanding our reasonably com-
prehensive knowledge of rabbit reproduction, puberty was
marked by sniggering, ignorance and rumour.

---

* Yes, reportedly. Because who would volunteer to compare and contrast all
the stingers in the insect world?

Remember the scene in *The Fly* when Jeff Goldblum's fingernails start to peel off? The near-hysterical panic he felt as his body began to morph? That's very much how I felt when my first pubic hair arrived. Cruelly, it turned up on its own, an advance party of one for whatever my body was planning next. For weeks, as it grew longer and longer, I worried that this might be it. I would be mono-pubed, doomed to a life in fairground trailers with bearded women and two-headed dogs. I experimented by folding it back over itself to create the impression of plurality, but that only served to add frizz. For a while that felt like an eternity, my foot-long pube was the talk of the changing room. If I could have swapped it for a glove full of bullet ants, I would have done. Then, seemingly overnight, a flanker in the B team developed a full ginger merkin and stole my unwanted limelight. He was teased mercilessly by the bald majority until other balls began to drop and the ridicule was redirected from the hirsute to the hairless.

With all these developments – the body hair, the stubble, the spots, the breaking voice – you didn't want to be first and you didn't want to be last. You wanted to be in the majority. Always. And so it was with skirmishes with the opposite sex. Nobody knew what they were doing. We just knew that we had to do it because everyone else was doing it (even though they weren't). Our coming of age was guided by fear, by the gulf between what we were told and sold on screen and our own pimply, sprouting, embarrassed reality, and by a desperate need to remain unremarkable. In the absence of celebratory initiations, of any sort of communal march to adulthood, adolescence was a dividing, individualistic process. It taught us to be ashamed of our bodies and of being different. It showed us that we were on our own.

Of course, we all get through it, just as (most) Sateré-Mawé kids get through their initiations, but I wonder how much of an impact it has on us in later life? All through this book, you will meet men who should be asking for help and should be sharing their feelings but choose to hide in a bath or block out their emotions. They share a certain reticence, a reluctance to display weakness. How much of this is instilled not only in the classroom but in our lonely initiation into adulthood?

Ridiculously, the closest we get to a formal recognition of maturity is the driving test. An elder takes you on a journey. Your capabilities are tested. Can you remain calm at a busy junction? Can you mirror, signal, manoeuvre? Can you execute a three-point turn? You get to the end of the test, the elder looks down at his clipboard and, with luck, shakes your hand and says, 'Congratulations, you've passed.' What you hear is: 'Congratulations, you are now a fully licensed grown-up.'

After an entire adolescence with responsibility largely abdicated to disciplinarian teachers and helicopter parents, with very little trust and a large dollop of mental, physical and socio-sexual anxiety, someone hands you the (car) key to adulthood. And how do we react? Badly, of course. In the UK, just 7 per cent of all licence holders are under twenty-five, but that age bracket accounts for nearly one-fifth of the drivers who are killed or seriously injured in crashes each year. Young men are far more likely to crash than young women. And seventeen-year-olds are up to four times more likely to die in a crash when carrying young passengers than when driving alone.

Perhaps these statistics would be less grim if we gave young men more of the educational latitude we discussed in the previous chapter and more guidance through the adolescent milestones we've discussed in this one. As it stands, we are sending boys into adulthood with a pressing need to prove themselves in a culture where there aren't many healthy ways to do that.

The first priority is to grow up when it comes to, snigger, sex. Forget the cornflakes. Move on from the residual alarmism that's still inherent in the way we explain the facts of life to our kids. A few years ago, researchers published an overview of sex education across Europe. The Nordic and Benelux countries fared best. Denmark – she of the magical forest school movement – has had mandatory sex education since 1970 and, since 1991, it has been integrated 'in all school subjects'. Pupils at primary and secondary stage are encouraged to ask questions about sex, gender or relationships 'at any time'. Each year, they consolidate all this with 'Sex Week'. Rather predictably, this is a whole week of sex education that covers not only the biology but also what it means to have a healthy relationship, both physically and mentally. The kids are even given homework to do with their parents. Last year, this comprised six discussions about the sharing of nude images online. Unsurprisingly, Denmark has the lowest teen pregnancy rate in Western Europe. Even more unsurprisingly, the UK has the highest.

The second priority is to make more of a boy's coming

of age. A can of finagled cider, an entirely fabricated sex life and the ability to navigate a three-point turn just won't cut it. A few years ago, I had just started my fifth decade and Freddie, still the apple of my eye, had just started his second. Bullet ants are hard to find in west Kent, and his mother was immovable on the cow's blood, so his godfather and I decided to take him to Dartmoor in early spring for a wild-camping adventure. It wasn't supposed to be too hardcore, too stoic, too Rudyard Kipling. He wasn't going to be packed off into the hills to find himself or die trying. But, as bad luck would have it, the trip coincided with a freakishly Baltic cold front sweeping unhelpfully across the West Country.

It was a bit snowy when we set off but the Met Office was already issuing amber warnings. We discussed turning back, but it was ultimately Freddie's decision and, because of his underdeveloped frontal lobe, he wanted to press on. His elders' frontal lobes were preoccupied with being middle-aged and desperately trying to prove they weren't, so we agreed. After a five-hour trek through increasingly horizontal snow, we pitched our two tiny tents in a full-scale blizzard. Now, to be clear, both of the adults in the party had expedition experience, and this was not a 'men rescued from Ben Nevis wearing only T-shirts and flip-flops' situation. We were well equipped and well prepared. Nevertheless, there was a point in the middle of that howling gale of a night when I was worried. It was minus ten outside the tent and not much warmer inside – cold enough to make sleep impossible, even after we'd cracked open the emergency turkey-roast blankets. So Freddie and I just lay there talking above the relentless, howling wind until dawn. Those conversations rather than the challenge were what mattered.

That morning, as we dug ourselves out of our nest and tried to stamp the cold from our limbs, it was clear that the adventure was over and that, in the midst of a whiteout, we had to get off the hills. Many quite tense hours later, not long after I'd called home and received a well-deserved dressing down ('I knew you shouldn't have gone'), the three of us were sitting by a pub fire, wondering how many toes we might lose, and planning the next year's trip.

This annual expedition – as it has become – won't necessarily ensure that Fred drives sensibly or leaves childhood with a healthier sense of what it means to be a man. It certainly won't guarantee that he'll approach romantic relationships with warmth and empathy rather than fear and shame ... although I hope our concerted efforts to be as Danish as possible with regard to sex and relationship education will help on that score.

The truth is that in the few short years that have passed since that first snowbound journey, he's already making his own path into adulthood. When I drop him off at the bus stop in the morning, he prefers me not to wave goodbye. When I meet his friends, I can cross the embarrassing-dad threshold with alarming ease just by being myself. The teenage shutters have come down, the suit of armour is on. All of this is normal and understandable – I'm always suspicious of those parents who describe their adolescent offspring as their 'best friends'. Although I like to think that Fred's move away is motivated by a desire for independence rather than a fear of dependence, I know that it will be a mix of the two. In order to be part of his peer group, he must take cues from that peer group. I just hope that it is enough for him to know that I'll be there if he needs me.

There should be a better way to honour a son's journey into adulthood, but until there is a seismic shift in British society and gender expectation, a combination of Dartmoor and Danishness is the best I've got. It is, at the very least, an improvement on a sliced penis on an overhead projector.

CHAPTER THREE

Men and adulthood

Dear Matt,

Don't freak out. This is me, your forty-five-year-old future self. I've found a hole in the space–time continuum and here I am. You and I need to have a serious talk, so please listen carefully. I know you think you're incredibly busy but, mate, you have no idea. Wait until you have three kids, which – I hope you're sitting down for this – you will. (Side note: don't spend three years arguing about how many is too many with your future wife. She wants three and three turns out to be a lot of fun, but you probably should have got on with it sooner. That way, you wouldn't still be fourteen years away from them all leaving home, would you? Idiot.)

Anyway, we were laughing at how busy you think you are. Wait until the idea of a night out, just for the hell of it, no planning, *que sera, sera*, seems about as unachievable as Leicester City winning the Premier League. (Which they do, by the way, in 2016. Don't tell anyone. Just put a tenner down at the start of the season. Trust me.) Wait until the most relaxing part of your day is the commute home, even though you never get a seat and the guy whose armpit within which your face is involuntarily nestled has his iPhone on really, really loud. (What's an iPhone? Like your iPod, only it means your boss can email, text and call you any time, day or night. It's fantastic.)

I know what you're thinking. You've got your whole life ahead of you. You've got a whole career to sort out. And you've got a deposit on a cupboard above a Post Office to save for. And you've got to find 'the one'. That's all good. I'm pretty sure it will work out fine. But I want you to stop and think about how you will feel in two decades' time. Let's assume everything does work out fine. If it does, *this* is how you will feel ...

First of all, you won't really care about how successful you are at work. You'll love your family and, because you are a man in a man's world, you'll still think, subconsciously but also, frequently, consciously, that it's your duty to provide for them. But, because you are what we used to call a 'New Man', but we now call 'a man', you will also want to *see* your family. You will want to earn your family cake and eat it. So, you'll try very hard to find some sort of work–life balance and you will fail. You will work from home some days, like you're some kind of dad hero, even though you actually work harder when you're there because you are, rightly, paranoid that people in the office call it *shirking* from home. You'll take almost all your annual leave. You'll leave the office when your work is done, not when it's so late that your boss asks, 'Why are you still here?' Big stuff like that. All good. Except those attempts to find a work–life balance will have been enough to mark you down as 'not a thrusting type'.

Unfortunately, there will be plenty of twenty-five-year-olds at work who are very happy to have no work–life balance whatsoever. They'll be highly motivated to climb the ladder and no one will be able to convince them that ladder-climbing isn't all it's cracked up to be. I'm not trying to convince you either, by the way. You can't just sit at the bottom of the ladder all your life, can you? I'm just asking you to think about it. Ambition isn't everything. Take some time to consider what makes you happy.

There are some other points, but I'll bullet them because I know you think you're busy. God, that's hilarious. I mean, what have you got to do today? Load a plate and a mug into a dishwasher? Rent a DVD? In eighteen years' time, here's what you'll do on a typical day before you get on the train to travel to the job that is no longer the most important thing in your life ... not by a long shot. You'll get dressed, get three children dressed, re-dress the youngest one because, somehow, he's going through a toddler fashionista phase and blue is so last season, wipe at least two bottoms, toilet-brush at least two toilets, toothbrush two sets of teeth, neither of which is yours, unload and load a whole dishwasher (two loads a day, my friend, not one a month), take a dog for a walk (you won't win on the third child, but you must, repeat must, put your foot down over the Border collie), feed some cats (same deal), make fourteen mind-numbingly dull but apparently critically important decisions about a new kitchen you can't afford (see Chapter Eight), drive a child to the bus stop because you thought it would be a good idea to move to the country (which it was, but, God, there's a lot of driving), walk two other children to another school, drive to a road that is two miles from the station but has free parking, then run those two miles because you're late, always late, for everything.

Anyway, the bullet points ...

- Cancel your gym membership. It's always a phase, you never stick at it, and by the time you hit forty you'll realise that all the cardio you were told was great throughout the first half of your life has actually knackered your knees. And your back. And, oddly, your little fingers. Just do twenty press-ups a day, eat more vegetables and fewer cornflakes (you know why they were invented, don't you?) and you'll be fine.
- Resist the temptation to buy a new CD player, a new MD player, a new Sonos system, a new Bose system or, indeed, any music-streaming device. Likewise, do not buy the iPhone, the iPhone 3G, 3GS, 4, 4S, 5, 5C, 5S, 6, 6 Plus, 6S, 6S Plus, SE, 7, 7 Plus, 8, 8 Plus, X, XS, XS Max or XR. Ditto 3D OLED televisions, computers, Wi-Fi range extenders, portable hard drives, Kindles, solar chargers and power blocks. All of these things are designed to make you unhappy (see Chapter Seven). Live by

one simple rule: do not buy any gadget that requires a new type of cable. Limit yourself to a simple phone, a small television, a basic laptop and a car that runs until it dies.

- In three years' time, someone called Mark Zuckerberg will invent something called Facebook. You have two options: travel to Cambridge, Massachusetts, and kill Zuckerberg before he can release this, the single most alienating aspect of twenty-first century life; or never open a Facebook account.

- DIY. Right now, you have a hard time building an IKEA Billy bookcase. You think this is acceptable. You think it's funny. You even wrote an article about it because you and everyone else in the media love to stereotype male uselessness. Sort yourself out. If you don't, you will spend the next two decades handing increasingly large amounts of cash to 'that'll-cost-you' workmen to do jobs you are perfectly capable of doing yourself. Step one: buy a drill with an Allen key bit. You'll be astonished how much easier this makes it to master the IKEA flatpack. You'll be like a Formula One tyre changer in no time. Step two: don't freak out when the hole you've drilled in the wall for the bookshelf you've decided you can construct is not exactly in line with the other hole. Take a deep breath. Don't cry. Don't start phoning estate agents. Fill in the hole and drill a new one an inch to the left. Easy. Step three: apply this approach to all DIY tasks. Be prepared to make a mistake. Understand that you can fix mistakes. Caveat: this does not apply to plumbing or electrical work. Even though you will go on a weekend plumbing course in four years' time and decide it's not that hard, it is. Know your limits.

- Your world will shrink as you get older. Just accept that this is beyond your control (although, nudge, you now know what to do about Mark Zuckerberg). Once you have children, it will become almost impossible to maintain any semblance of a social life (no, the NCT group doesn't count). Make time for good friends and ditch bad ones. Always send physical Christmas cards. Never send birthday greetings via Facebook (again, see above). Enjoy the crumbs of fun you are left with.

- What is the point of it all? Your forty-five-year-old self has begun to comprehend what your eighty-year-old self will know for a fact: working for the sake of status and money is pointless. You will never have enough of either. There will always be another rung on the ladder, always something or someone to covet, always a newer smartphone (oooh, look, *three* cameras). Enjoy the present, not the presents.

- Buy shares in Facebook.

- And a PS from mid-2020: don't take restaurants for granted, hug your parents, hug everyone and never, ever panic about toilet rolls. There will always be enough. I know that doesn't make sense now, but it's better that way. Just trust me, particularly about the toilet rolls.

I had two serious accidents in my twenties, both of which should have made me stop and take stock, although neither did, for reasons I shall outline below.

The second accident happened on a back road in Pennsylvania at ten o'clock at night, right at the end of the last millennium. I was a young, aspiring travel writer behind the wheel of a rented red Mustang heading to a bed and breakfast in the boondocks. If I had taken a moment to think about it, which I definitely didn't, life could not have been better.

As I came around a long, sweeping corner, I glimpsed a large motorbike pulling directly into my path and, before I could react, the entire front of the car disintegrated. Airbags exploded. The noise was incredible. When I clambered out of the half a car that was left, I saw the twisted remains of a Harley Davidson about thirty yards back. Beyond that, its owner was lying twisted and motionless. Another twenty yards back, I found a woman lying equally still, a pool of dark blood forming around her head. Neither of them had been wearing a crash helmet and it was immediately obvious that I had just killed two people.

I started to call for help as a large group of hairy bikers poured out of the adjacent roadside pub. A few of them started yelling, 'Find the driver, this is a crime scene.' I yelled back, 'I am the driver. Call nine–one–one.' Within minutes, two local news helicopters had arrived at the scene, their spotlights illuminating the appalling carnage. After what seemed like many more hours but was probably only minutes, an army of ambulances, police cars and breakdown trucks had also arrived to try to help the victims and pacify the angry bikers.

To cut a grim story short, I hadn't been speeding or drinking or taking unnecessary risks. That much cannot be said of the guy who had pulled out of the pub car park with no lights and no warning. The Harley had gone under the car, the two riders over the top. It had taken me a few seconds – which will remain with me for the rest of my life – to realise that the pool of blood around the girl's head was actually a red scarf. She survived relatively – miraculously – unscathed, although I wouldn't find that out until much later. The biker had a broken leg. Given the level of devastation on the road, I will never understand how they were so lucky. The local sheriff, after breathalysing all three of us, was kind enough to point out that being very, very drunk tends to increase the chances of survival.

I was checked over in the back of one of the ambulances and asked if I wanted to go to hospital. I said I was fine because that's what you say when there are other people with more serious injuries. Of course, I wasn't fine. I was in a state of deep shock and had a strange numbness in my arms. But I was also a young, aspiring travel writer who had a story with which to be getting on.

I was due to meet a representative of the Pennsylvania Tourist Board the following afternoon. Hardly Watergate, but it had taken me years to find an actual job at an actual travel magazine, so I wasn't about to cry off just because my arms were tingling. Having established that I wasn't a murderer, the owner of the pub said I could stay there until the morning. I was too traumatised to think up a better plan, so I spent a sleepless, increasingly tearful night on a strange, stained sofa-bed in a strange, stained storage room looking through a flickering neon sign to the road where I had – unbelievably – not killed two people.

The next morning, I took a taxi ninety miles to the bed and breakfast where I should have stayed the night before. There, parked on the street outside, was the Mustang I'd smashed to smithereens. Or rather, an identikit replacement. Same colour, same spec, same rental sticker, like nothing had happened. Honestly, that was the worst part of the whole horror show. It would have been better if the trip had been ruined. It would have been better to go to hospital, rather than spend the next six months in increasing pain due to the two vertebrae it eventually turned out I had fractured. I now see that rented Mustang – magically restored, like an eight-valve, four-litre Terminator – as a metaphor for my twenties. I didn't stop and think. I didn't take a breath. Like a lost man who won't pull over and ask for directions, I just carried on regardless.

The first accident of my twenties was more serious (for me, that is – the guy on the Harley might disagree). But the way I dealt with it was pretty much identical to how the rental company dealt with the Mustang: as if nothing had happened.

I had spent my teenage years as a classical music nerd. I played the piano badly and the bassoon rather well. I hadn't decided on a particular career when I went to university, but the two preferred options were some form of writing and some form of music. I was never going to be a virtuoso bassoonist. Virtuoso bassooning is quite the niche sport. But I loved playing in orchestras. I loved mucking about at the back in the nine-hundred-bar rests you get when you're third bassoon, then nailing the four-bar solo in the second movement. I knew I would be quite content cracking viola jokes with the clarinets in a regional orchestra for the next few decades.

But that half-plan went out of the window, literally, at the very beginning of university. The week after freshers' week, a girl asked me to open the window in question. She couldn't budge it and nor could I, but because I am a man, and in such moments all consideration, forethought, intelligence and common sense are instantly and irredeemably obliterated by knuckle-dragging ego, I started banging it with my fist. The glass broke, my arm went through, and when I pulled it back in surprise, I sliced through most of the important tubes in my wrist.* Blood and synovial fluid sprayed everywhere.

This time, I did go to the hospital. Two in fact. One very delicate operation later, the surgeon told me I would never regain the feeling in half of my right hand and had lost all of the lateral movement in my fingers. But he was a glass-half-full kind of guy – another couple of millimetres, he explained, and I would have lost the hand altogether so, really, this was a good thing. I was less chirpy. Ten thousand hours of bassooning, all for nothing.

The last concert in which I would ever perform featured Mozart's *Requiem*. Mozart was a big fan of the bassoon. In the *Requiem*, before the choir starts warbling, before

---

* If you ever punch through a pane of glass, leave your arm where it is. Don't pull it back. Just leave it hanging there. You'll do much less damage. And I said this wasn't a self-help book.

the strings start rising, before the oboes ruin the whole thing, there is a single, beautiful, mournful introductory melody ... and Mozart gave it to the bassoon.* So, I got to start a whole concert. Then, a few weeks later, I chopped off most of my hand.

Here's how I dealt with this huge event in my life. I had a bit of a cry when I woke up in the recovery room, largely because Mum had listened to me telling her I was just calling home to say I'd had a bit of an accident and I needed a bit of surgery, but I was fine and I'd call her again when I was out of theatre, nothing to worry about, everything's great, byeee ... and as soon as the call was over, she'd driven more than three hundred miles straight through the night to be at my bedside when I came round. Mums always know.

I was quite morose for the next few days in hospital. I had been looking forward to college life, the freedom of it, the fun. On a very basic level, I had swapped single-sex secondary education for co-ed tertiary education. There were girls ... and parties with girls. It was all very grown-up and exciting. Finally, I was in charge of my own destiny. And I'd marked this momentous moment, this great step into maturity, by demonstrating that I couldn't be trusted with windows.

Discharged a week later, I told my tutors I wouldn't be able to study music any more and would like to switch to history. Fine, they said, and that was that. With one slit of the wrist, I'd lost something I was passionate about,

---

* Okay, there's a clarinet in there too, but the bassoon carries the tune.

that I'd focused on since the age of eleven and that could have been an integral part of my adult life. Now it was gone for ever. Fine, I agreed and, without giving it another thought, popped down to the library to order some books on Weimar Germany.

Over the next three years, I played backgammon, drank cheap sherry, wrote essays in late-night panics and grew increasingly tired of my Ronseal nickname, 'One Point Five Hands'. Then I graduated. Then I applied for jobs. Then, eventually, I got one. No hesitation, repetition or deviation.

The *Just a Minute* approach is very much the order of the day in early adulthood. You've spent somewhere between thirteen and sixteen years, maybe longer, in formal, prescriptive, monitored and regulated education. You've ticked all the boxes, jumped through all the hoops, and your prospects in life have been reduced to grades on a piece of paper. Now, you have to get on with it. Exactly what 'it' might be is probably still undecided, but that's not as important as the 'getting on' part. Why? Because of deficiency motivators.

In his 1954 book *Motivation and Personality*, the brilliant psychologist Abraham Maslow* described a hierarchy of five motivators: physiological (hunger, thirst, shelter, sex), safety (protection from physical and emotional harm), social (friendship, acceptance, affection), esteem (a.k.a. ego)

---

* As (one of) the father(s) of humanistic psychology, Maslow's focus was far more enthusiastic and far less Oedipal than Freud's. He believed humans could change of their own volition and that not everything was dictated by what happened to you as a child. He advocated a more positive approach to life, rather than treating everyone 'like a bag of symptoms'.

and, right at the top of the pyramid, self-actualisation. A self-actualised person is a great person. His perception of reality is closer to actual reality. He is comfortable with himself and others. He is open to different experiences and empathetic to other people's problems. He is creative and capable not only of profound relationships but also of spontaneity. In short, what a guy. He is the friend you invite to your birthday party and then complain about afterwards because everyone loved him so much.

Of course, it's not easy becoming that guy. Level Five is the black belt of motivators – only possible, Maslow argues, once you've achieved all the other levels. Critically, it is different from the first four because it's a growth motivator rather than a deficiency motivator. In other words, it's not about satisfying urgent needs but about becoming a better person.

This fifth level is absolutely key to understanding what happens in midlife. Indeed, it is only in midlife that many men start to become aware of it, or at least start to suspect that there is more to life than satisfying more materialistic needs. But the process of self-actualisation is not clear or obvious. It can all become quite existentialist quite quickly. What is the point of my life? Why am I here? What is my purpose? These are the Augean questions some men start to ask themselves and other men try, sensibly, to block out. Either way, consciously or subconsciously, there is a creeping sense that the first four levels are no longer enough. There must be more.

I'll come back to Maslow's level-five black belt in later chapters, but for now, we're in our twenties.

Self-actualisation is still a long way off.* We just have to focus on the basics.

In some respects, Maslow's hierarchy follows the human life cycle. Babies are preoccupied with stages one and two – they're hungry, they're thirsty and they want to feel secure. Toddlers totter up to level three because they want social interaction, and teenagers are still there because they're obsessed with fitting in. Young adults who crave status have made it to level four. Then, if you're an optimist … *Ta-da!* You progress to maturity and self-actualisation. It's a nice, linear, manageable concept, but it ignores what it's really like to be a young adult. When you venture out into the real world, it feels like you have nothing. You're at the start of the proper life cycle. You're no longer told what to do by parents and teachers. You're out there on your own. You're motivated by a whole host of deficiencies.

For a start, you're still physiologically deficient. Oh yes you are. You're living like Withnail in a rented bedsit in a part of town the estate agent described, criminally, as 'up and coming'. As for sex, it's infrequent and still not anything like as professional as it is in the movies or as available as it is on *Love Island*.

Level two – safety – is not under control, either. On a very basic level, rates of violent crime victimhood are highest

---

* It needn't be this way. The more we understand why so many men end up miserable, the sooner we can take action. It's not inevitable that the start of adult life is all about climbing ladders with no consideration of creating lasting happiness. We're in a transition phase now – half or a third of the way from old-fashioned, stoic, miserable manhood to new, balanced, fallible, happy manhood. And we'll get there. Perhaps not in time for my generation, perhaps not by the end of this book, but we will get there.

among young men. Today, in our increasingly unequal society, this manifest itself most bleakly in the rise in street crime and the growing numbers of young men who feel the need to carry a knife 'for protection'. Back when the current crop of middle-aged men was starting out, it just meant you never looked anyone in the eye on a night out; and, while not looking anyone in the eye, if you spilt their pint, you immediately offered to buy all their drinks for the rest of the evening. And when you walked home to your bedsit in the up-and-coming area, you did so quickly and nervously, trying to ignore all the yellow incident boards along the way: '7/9/97 approximately 10.20 a.m. Man and dog stabbed. Did you see or hear anything?'*

As for the third tier – socialisation – well, you're starting from scratch again. Where you ended up in the playground pecking order is irrelevant. Your friends are dispersing (as, thank God, are your enemies). The brutally simple structures of childhood are being replaced by a more fluid, unpredictable social existence. You're probably also single. If so, you are motivated not to be single. You must find 'the one' or 'a one'. Then, at some point, you must work out how slides one and two lead to slide three in that half-forgotten biology lesson and reproduce. All of this seems like a very tall order at the start of your twenties.

Not that there is anything wrong with these motivations. This is a fun time. You're free – at last – from the stresses

---

* A real sign, I promise, outside my eight-bedrooms-squeezed-into-a-four-bed-semi bedsit the week I moved in. The stabbed man was bad enough but the dog too?

of childhood. You can do anything you want and you've
got all the time in the world in which to do it. This is precisely why 'you've got your whole life ahead of you' is such
a well-worn phrase. Life is an adventure and, finally, you
can get on with it.

There is, however, the fourth tier in Maslow's motivational growth cake – esteem. And it's here that we find
the source of what will eventually lead to unhappiness,
anxiety and, if you're really unfortunate, a full-blown
midlife crisis. If childhood is when we are indoctrinated
into equating exam results with success, and success with
happiness, then early adulthood can come as a shock to
the system. Suddenly, we're starting again and all the gold
stars for good behaviour, the rewards for self-regulation,
are replaced with a whole new set of far vaguer metrics. Or,
as one geography graduate who now works in IT puts it:
'None of it amounted to anything ... What a waste of time.'

Employers don't care how much you know about the War
of the Roses or how succinctly you can explain what the
bloody lighthouse represents in *To the Bloody Lighthouse*.
They're looking for attributes like character, resilience,
communication skills and, for the first year at least, three in
my case, how well you can make a cup of tea. You're back
on the bottom rung of a whole new ladder. Or in a bucket
somewhere beneath the ladder that companies call 'graduate training'. Or, if you're mad enough to set your sights on
a creative industry, in a photocopying room with no obvious access to any ladder. This is called 'work experience'.

'I did everything that was expected of me at school,' says
Dan, a forty-four-year-old who, on paper, has led a rather

glamorous, enviable life. 'I passed all my exams and I graduated with a first from one of the best universities in the country. I was, according to my tutors, "top drawer", "destined for great things". I arrived in London feeling very full of myself. I even decided to be quite picky when deciding to whom I would offer my clearly impressive services. They would, after all, be lucky to have me. It took five long years of menial work, crazy hours and blatant exploitation before I finally understood that I was not the catch I thought I was.'

When I ask Dan why the dawning of this realisation took so long, he says, 'I probably knew within a few months, but my ego wouldn't let me admit it for much, much longer.'

Dan had chosen to work in the film industry. He started as a runner and gradually worked his way up to the position of producer on the television dramas the rest of us try to stay awake for on Sunday nights. He is, by society's standards, a stellar success. Except his entire twenties were spent working the sort of hours with which a junior doctor could empathise. His diet was unhealthy, his work–life balance non-existent, his commitment to his career unwavering.

'I was on a shoot for the first four months of my daughter's life,' he says. 'I had to leave my father's funeral early to catch a flight.' When I ask why he always put work first, he shrugs and looks despondent. 'I think, when I started, I expected it would be easier. I'd worked so hard at school and then at university and I thought that would mean something. When it became apparent that it didn't, I suppose I could have tried something else. But the longer it went on, the more there was to lose. There were always people who were willing to work longer and harder. If you didn't make the sacrifice, others gladly would. So I just kept going. I never seriously considered stopping until, one morning, I just couldn't get out of bed.'

At the age of forty-one, more or less a stranger to his family, Dan ground to a halt. After forty-eight hours of total lethargy, his wife convinced him to go to the doctor, who convinced him to seek help for depression and alcohol addiction. Three years on, he is still recovering ... and he no longer works in television. Was it worth it? 'No,' he says, very firmly. 'But I don't think I would have done it differently. I don't think that was even an option. If you want to be successful, you have to work hard. I don't think I would be where I am now, valuing life, with a far healthier perspective on status and success, without first experiencing the other side of it.'

By the time I got my first proper job – as an editorial assistant on a small travel magazine – I had already been entirely disabused of any notion that my academic qualifications amounted to anything in the real world. I had spent two years on two continents doing bits and pieces of work experience and a mountain of data entry. I had also spent a whole summer phoning the owners of a certain model of car to tell them that it might catch fire. Because this was the fifth time these customers had been told their cars might catch fire, they did not thank me for my potentially life-saving call. Several times a day, I made someone so angry that I could leave the call, walk to the kitchen, make a cup of tea and return to find they still hadn't finished telling me precisely what they thought of me, the company and my mother.

So you can imagine my delight when I landed that first proper job. It didn't matter that the only reason I got it – as the publisher never ceased to remind me – was because I was the only one of the forty applicants who ordered a pint in the pub-garden interview and nothing to do with my suspiciously long and glittering CV. It also didn't matter that the job in question was mostly admin, that it paid less than the car-fire 'you're-an-asshole' gig and that I had to live in the cheapest bedsit in all of Acton with three mature students, a drug dealer, two unemployed art graduates and a fifty-something alcoholic ghost of Christmas future who spent most nights having imaginary arguments with his ex-wife. None of that mattered, because I was *on the ladder.* And I would do anything to stay on it. I would work the longest hours. I would test forty outdoor jackets in a supermarket cool room.* I would eat tinned spaghetti five nights a week. I would fracture two vertebrae and just carry on like nothing had happened.

Of the many middle-aged professionals who have dropped their guards and confided in me for this book, very few paint a pretty picture of their early careers. On the face of it, that's understandable. You can't expect to start a career and have all the fun stuff immediately. You have to work your way up. You have to earn your corner office, your desk with its Newton's cradle, your place in the upper echelons of the professional world.

What is most striking about this process is not how relentless it is, but how little time we devote to thinking

---

* (And find the ones I tested first the warmest – durr!)

about what awaits us at the end of it. Recovering alcoholic and recovering television producer Dan might well be correct when he claims you can't find happiness in midlife without experiencing unhappiness in the decade or so prior to midlife, but it's ridiculous that we don't stop and think about this stuff until we are forced to do so.

Last year, the Junior Lawyers Division's Resilience and Wellbeing Survey – which quizzed students, graduates, trainee solicitors and solicitors with up to five years on the job – found that 93 per cent of respondents felt stressed. More than half said they had experienced poor mental health. That's an astonishingly high figure, particularly when you consider that law is a highly desirable profession. It's not like being a traffic warden or a debt collector. People go to great lengths to become lawyers. So it's not ideal that more than half of them find, on realising their deeply held ambition, that it comes with an accompanying mental health crisis.

Medical professionals have it even worse. A 2011 report in the *British Medical Journal* found that a third of doctors have a mental health disorder. Six years later, the Royal College of Physicians reported that 80 per cent of junior doctors felt their work put them under excessive stress. A quarter believed that this was having a significant impact on their mental health.

Adam Kay documented his miserable time as a junior doctor in his best-selling diary, *This is Going to Hurt*. His midlife crisis came earlier than most: he left the NHS in 2010, at the age of twenty-nine, after what he described, with characteristic understatement, as 'a bad day'. Newly promoted to senior registrar, he had to step in when a

Caesarean started to go wrong. He was unable to save the baby and, after a desperate battle, the mother ended up in intensive care. 'Everyone at the hospital was very kind to me and said all the right things,' he wrote. 'And yet, at the same time, it felt a bit like I'd sprained my ankle. There was the definite expectation that I'd still come into work the next day, the reset button firmly pressed.'

Kay opted for an alternative approach. He left medicine, left the ladder he'd put so much effort into climbing and started again on a very different ladder – writing and performing comedy. It's a classic – if extreme – midlife story, albeit a decade earlier than most people start experiencing theirs.

At the time, Kay didn't tell anyone – including his father (also a doctor), his mother and his partner – the real reason why he resigned. Ten years later, he admits to me, 'I wasn't in a great place. I hadn't recovered. You're just expected to carry on. I couldn't and then, suddenly, I wasn't a doctor any more. I had lost my personality-defining trait. My first Christmas out of medicine was rotten. It was like I'd come back from the army. I was lost and bewildered. I don't know if I had PTSD, but if I didn't, I had something close. I was regularly waking up sweating, pulse racing, back in that operating theatre. As far as my body was concerned, I was back there.

'There is evidence about how to cope with a traumatic experience,' he continues. 'There's evidence for talking to people, there's evidence for tea, for mindfulness, for taking time out, all sorts of things, and doctors are generally evidence-based. They don't diagnose on a whim. But when it comes to this, there is no self-care.'

This prompts an obvious question: why didn't he tell his partner (now his husband), James? Kay shakes his head. 'It was just a massive thing that I didn't talk about,' he says. 'And as the years went on, it became less and less relevant that I didn't. My brain was making me think about it – think about it more than I wanted to think about it. I was never going to volunteer to talk about it. It felt like a failure.'

Four years ago, he decided to read extracts from his diaries at the Edinburgh Festival in support of striking junior doctors. 'I did some preview shows in Islington and told my funny stories,' he says. 'I thought I was painting a picture, a death by a thousand cuts. But everyone just said, "I don't really understand why you left."' The next night, he did the show again, but this time told everyone – including James – about his final traumatic case. 'The audience left feeling awful, but it was good for me,' he says, laughing. 'It all came out and I cried.'

Later, when I mention this to James, he recalls that he was furious because it had taken Adam six years to find his emotional honesty. And his other loved ones all wondered why he hadn't told them earlier. I don't find his reticence surprising at all. It was exactly the same psychological reaction as Dan's refusal to seek help until he found himself lying catatonic in bed for forty-eight hours straight. Both of them opted for the bottling-up approach.

When I ask Kay why he went into medicine in the first place, he describes it as a largely inexorable process. He attended Dulwich College – all boys, plenty of exam pressure, 'single-sex education needs to go' – and felt it was more or less inevitable that he would follow in his father's footsteps. 'I was funnelled into medicine,' he says. 'I realised I didn't adore med school, but by then it was too late. It would have been such a failure to admit that it wasn't necessarily for me.'

He suggests the narrow specialisation that is medical school should be delayed until after a more general degree, as it is in the United States, because an eighteen-year-old might not be ready to decide if they are suited to the intense and emotionally turbulent life of a doctor. (Tube drivers have 'more of a psych eval' before starting the job, he adds.) Failing that, admittance to medical school should be based on more than 'good grades and a proficiency at the cello'.

Just like Adam Kay, we are all, to varying degrees, funnelled. We make life decisions based on what other people think, what other people expect, what society considers appropriate and what our exam grades allow us to do. Unless those decisions happen to align with what genuinely motivates us, at some point, we're going to come unstuck.

Of course, it's very easy to tell young people – and young men in particular – to make considered life decisions and take the time to evaluate every factor, but why on earth would they listen to us? Even if they did, what are these factors and how should they evaluate them? I can't imagine my twenty-five-year-old self paying much attention to my forty-five-year-old thoughts on the meaning of life. I remember feeling quite superior to my friends back then. Many of them were earning far more than me, but they were either racking up insane hours in law firms, hospitals and management consultancies or they'd donned the pinstripes and marched off to the City. 'Imagine being motivated by money,' I thought dismissively. 'How shallow.' But what were *my* motivations? They were hardly altruistic. I loved telling people I was a writer. Nothing made me happier than to see my name in print. Or, to be more specific and even more pathetic, nothing made me happier than when other people saw my name in print. My City friends were driven by money. I was driven by bylines. Neither is great and neither is sustainable.

There have been mutterings that times are changing. The next generation is supposedly much more focused on maintaining a proper work–life balance. They are unwilling just to get on with it come rain or shine, unwilling to slog away at unrewarding tasks in order to make their way up some futile career ladder. Accordingly, they are labelled 'snowflakes', as if hesitating in the face of exploitation is a bad thing. Would it really be so awful if tomorrow's midlifers had somehow, magically, realised where they were heading and had taken steps to avoid it? Unfortunately, despite what the in-my-day brigade claim, they haven't.

None of the millennials and Generation Zers I've interviewed could be described as snowflakes. Compared to us, they're working longer hours in less secure jobs with more debt. The pressure to succeed has increased and it starts earlier. Children as young as thirteen are encouraged to focus on 'what they want to do when they grow up', and not in a fun 'astronaut or fireman' way, but more along the lines of: 'If you want to be an accountant, you should attend the lunchtime maths booster.' Careers fairs kick in at sixteen.

Following the lumpen arrival of tuition fees, market forces now swirl around our universities. Students, understandably, demand value for money. They want more lectures, more tutor contact and more vocational experience. The universities respond with CV workshops, mock interviews and a carousel of trade events. What was once an opportunity for deeper study and, let's be honest, considerable loafing has become an entirely practical, linear bridge between school and employment. League tables of employability are published to help students work out if £50,000-plus of debt is worth it. Would-be philosophers, artists and psychologists are faced with the bleak but inescapable fact that dentistry is a far more sensible option.

I am acutely aware that I write this from the luxurious vantage point of a pre-tuition-fees graduate. It took me a mere nine years to pay off my student loan, so it would be infuriating if I sat here on my debt-free high horse and told students to ignore the issues of employability and earning potential. So I won't, not entirely. But there should be some balance. Consider, by all means, the economic viability of a degree but don't consider it in isolation. Think about what brings you joy, what stirs your passion, what makes you happy – all that wishy-washy stuff that doesn't seem like a priority when you're staring at a telephone-number debt and you're being constantly reminded that you'll never pay it off studying the performing arts. If, after all that, the answer is still dentistry, good luck to you and your fortunate patients. If it isn't, Billy Elliot, do something else. Or just relax. Forget about a career for now. Don't, under any circumstances, attend a careers fair in freshers' week. You have the rest of your life to work. Enjoy the degree you chose because you love the subject ... or hate it less than all the other subjects. Wait for something exciting to come along. Wait for the epiphany. Use that narrow window of freedom between school and the grind of adult life wisely. Take. Your. Time.

All of which sounds like terrible advice to Patrick – a thoughtful, twenty-one-year-old English graduate. He tells me he feels enormous pressure to find a job. Although his parents sound enlightened – they want him to be happy, don't want him to spend his life doing something for the wrong reasons, want him to take his time and find the right path – there is still an expectation. Family friends repeatedly ask what he's doing, and he's increasingly embarrassed to tell them he hasn't decided yet.

The way he describes his situation, it sounds like he's been living in career purgatory for years, idling away his time in a backpacking, festival-going, surf-bumming sea of nothingness. Which would be fine, by the way. But he graduated only nine weeks ago.

'Many of my friends went straight into work and those of us who haven't are worried,' he says, chewing a nail to illustrate his point. 'I know several people who are considering doing a "panic master's" just so they can kick the can down the road again. It won't necessarily help their employment prospects, but it will mean people stop asking what they're doing with their lives.'

When I ask about his priorities, he says he wants a challenging career that 'will eventually lead to a decent wage and some status'. What about happiness? 'We don't talk a lot about that,' he says. 'There's a sense that happiness will come later.'

It feels cruel to point out that most of my middle-aged interviewees also regard happiness as a mid- to long-term – rather than imminent – prospect. A quick flick through my notebook and I see: 'If I can get through the next three years, the pressure will ease,' from a thirty-eight-year-old senior sales executive, and 'I've just got to stick with it [the job with its hellish dawn commute] until the mortgage is more manageable, then I can afford to take more risks,' appropriately enough from a forty-nine-year-old property manager. By 'more risks', he means more time for himself and with his family. Then there's the fifty-year-old fourth-sector worker who has been talking, seriously, about taking a six-month sabbatical to go and live in Argentina. 'We started planning it soon after we got married,' he says. 'Then we had kids. Then we started talking about it again once they were out of nappies. The oldest is now doing his GCSEs, so the new plan is to go next summer.' They won't go next summer. He knows that. Even as he's explaining the plan, with a level of conviction that stretches to showing me the website of a riding school outside Buenos Aires, he knows it. Happiness will always be just beyond the next pampas.

Patrick's response to these unfulfilled dreams is muted. He is dismissive of Generation Xers who tell him and his fellow twentysomethings to seize the day: 'It doesn't apply to us. We can't afford to do whatever we please. Not when we're just starting out.' The trouble is, seizing the day – or even just a couple of hours of it – doesn't get any easier. We become more risk-averse. Our responsibilities deepen as our options narrow.

But Patrick won't listen. He doesn't equate his status as a young, single man with freedom. Instead, he sees deficiencies. 'My friends and I don't do very much for the sake of here and now,' he concludes. 'We spend more time considering the future. We assume that once we get on the right career path and start progressing, then everything else – money, property, friends, love – will slot into place. Right now, we've got to prove ourselves. We need to establish new roots. Then, in five or ten years, we might be happy.'

An afterthought about thought

I know this is getting dangerously close to one of those boxes you get at the end of each chapter in a self-help book. But before we proceed, I just want to explain to my twenty-five-year-old self and other ladder-climbers what I mean when I say, 'Take more time to consider what makes you happy.' I don't have a complete answer because I'm still trying to work all of this out. But I have started to acquire some of the tools to find it. So, here goes ...

There is a tendency, instilled in our schooling and nurtured through the competition that is adult life, to be constantly doing things. We must have goals, tick lists, targets and, if we're a real nut, a spread-sheeted five-year plan. It is remarkably rare that we just do nothing. I don't mean Netflix nothing or whole-loaf-of-Marmite-toast nothing or whole-afternoon-on-Facebook nothing or build-a-blanket-fort-even-when-you-don't-have-kids nothing. I mean nothing, absolutely nothing – sitting on a sofa, or under a tree, or next to a river, or at least fifty yards from your phone not doing anything. If you try it, it can be almost painful: the sheer, anarchic pointlessness of it.

For me, this comes from worrying about what other people think. I'm constantly ready for someone to ask, 'How's work?' or 'How's life?' The answer is always 'Fine, thanks,' but in order to make it convincing, I need my work – or my life – to read like something an excessively proud parent would put in a Christmas round-robin: 'Everything's going amazingly well. I'm doing all of this and all of that. It's all so fabulous. Don't ask me any more questions or I might burst into tears. Cheerio.' I'm exaggerating, but only a little. I have a story – a story in which I am doing just fine, thank you very much – and I would hate it if anyone even suspected that story was fiction. This is why I find it so hard to do nothing. It feels virtually criminal. It's exhausting.

I am not alone. Men have been conditioned from the very beginning to be on the road to somewhere. Everything has to have a purpose. Were I to suggest to my twenty-five-year-old self that he should take more time to consider what makes him happy, he would nod sagely, whip out a notebook and start listing the things that make him happy. This would get him nowhere, because the important part is the taking more time, not the list. Slow down. Quieten your completer–finisher mind. Try to listen to your heart. That's what my wife – who is at least a blue belt in meditation – has been trying to persuade me to do for the last five years. It's only very recently that I've started to listen to her. Because what does 'listen to your heart' even mean?

It means ignoring the story you're telling yourself, the story that's built on your own and everyone else's expectations. Ignore the voice in your head that tells you to keep striving for some distant future goal. Chuck all of that out and just try to feel what's left.

The first time I gave this a proper go, a black hole of desolation opened up and I was so panicked that I didn't try again for months. Instead, I scurried back to the security of compiling lists. The second time felt slightly less disorientating. I managed to still my thoughts a little and did not end up dwelling on the utter pointlessness of existence. The third time, I became a Jedi master. I sat cross-legged in the garden one morning, closed my eyes, dismantled the narrative of my life and found happiness in the birdsong. I felt timeless, transported, free. When I opened my eyes, I expected it to be evening or next week or five decades later, but evidently only ten minutes had passed. I don't know what was going on there. Maybe it was something I ate.

All of this may sound ridiculous – especially the heartlistening – but it has helped me. Because these brief escapes give your true self – the one that usually suffocates under all the constructed versions of yourself – a little oxygen. Take a breath. Switch off your phone. Stop thinking for a minute or two …

Okay, now you can carry on reading. Or not. That's the point.

CHAPTER FOUR

Men and babies

As he read the text – 'Waters broke come now' – Peter took a deep breath and reminded himself that everything was ready. He had attended the NCT course with his wife, Sarah, and learnt that a contraction was like the reverberation of an electric guitar, which sounded manageable. He had memorised Sarah's ensuing six-page birth plan and printed it in triplicate, just in case. A home birth, then, to the soothing sounds of narwhals, illuminated by candles (scented or unscented, depending on her mood). No problem. With a nod to his colleagues as he ran for the lift, Peter's two weeks of paternity leave had begun. It was Monday afternoon.

By the small hours of Friday morning, many, many guitar strums later, the fifth, maybe sixth pair of midwives was clocking on. Both kinds of candle had burnt to the quick, the rented birthing pool was deflating in the dining room and after six, then eight, then nine, then back to seven centimetres of dilation, it was clear that all six pages of the birth plan were going out the window.

'We should go to hospital,' said one of the midwives, not for the first time. This time, though, having exhausted reserves of strength she didn't know she possessed, Sarah agreed. An ambulance, gas, air, an epidural and an emergency Caesarean later, their son George was finally born that evening.

'Even though I hadn't slept all week, I felt completely elated,' Peter says. 'It was such a long labour and then so urgent and frightening at the end, I really thought I was going to lose her. The fact that she was okay and George was okay just felt like a miracle.'

Months later, and only in the company of other dads, Peter dared to admit that he had found the birth hard. 'Don't say that in front of my wife,' said another dad. But they all quietly agreed that Peter was right. There is nothing worse (for a man, at any rate) than watching helplessly as your partner goes through a traumatic labour.

Peter spent the first five days of fatherhood driving in a constant loop from home to shops to maternity ward and back, delighting in the fact that he could finally do something useful. Then, on the Wednesday afternoon, having pro-wrestled the baby seat into the car with no help from the indecipherable instructions, he drove his new family home. When he thinks back to that moment, he smiles and becomes emotional. 'When I'd got them through the front door and they were in our bedroom, together, and George was having a feed, well . . . ' he begins, 'I don't think I'll ever be that happy again. They were safe. They were home. It was just amazing.' For the next seventy-two hours, Sarah looked after the baby and Peter looked after Sarah. Then, before they had even begun to master the art of parenting, before they'd started to process what had happened, what was happening and what was going to happen, Peter was back at his desk.

'How did it go?' asked a colleague on the way to a meeting in which Peter would struggle to stay awake. The previous fortnight – with all the blood, gore, screaming, crying, terror, panic and finally, mercifully, unadulterated joy – flashed before him. 'Fine,' he said eventually, because where would you start? 'All good.'

That afternoon, his colleagues presented him with a supermarket cake, but it's the thought that counts. He had planned to leave early, but another meeting in which he also struggled to stay awake overran.

In 2015, to great fanfare, the coalition government announced new rights for UK parents. Maternity leave became the more politically correct 'shared parental leave' (SPL), which meant both parents could now share up to fifty weeks of leave, thirty-seven of them paid. 'The Liberal Democrats want to tear down the barriers that stop people reaching their full potential,' declared the deputy prime minister, Nick Clegg. 'For too long, mums have been told their place is at home with their child while dads return to work. I want parents to choose for themselves how to balance work and family.'

Had we suddenly become all Scandinavian? Sadly not,

because Clegg's plan left parents with a Sophie's choice. If a dad wanted to take time off in the early months, those days would simply be deducted from the mum's allowance. This wasn't valuing the role of fathers, it was devaluing the role of mothers. In practice, none of that mattered much anyway. The legal change meant little for most new families. The vast majority of employers still paid just a week or two of full salary. After that, you got the statutory state handout of £145.18 a week.

In February 2018, the Department for Business realised that only 2 per cent of couples were taking advantage of the new rules. Politicians decided it must be an awareness issue so they launched a publicity campaign with the puke-inducing strapline 'Share the Joy'. But none of the new dads I interview are unaware of SPL. They simply could not afford to stay at home for more than a fortnight.

Chris, a thirty-nine-year-old environmental consultant, describes the safe arrival of his daughter at the end of 2018 as 'mind-blowing'. His wife had suffered a miscarriage in 2017 and was induced at thirty-five weeks. They spent their first week as a family – half his paid paternity leave – in the Transitional Care Unit at Worcester Royal Hospital. 'The baby was in an incubator, having phototherapy to treat jaundice,' he says. 'We could only really have her out to feed her via the nasal gastric tube. The nurses offered to do it for us, but we had so little contact with her, we learnt to do it ourselves.'

Once they were safely home, they started on the home-made meals Chris had stockpiled in the freezer ('to allow more time to enjoy our bundle of joy'). After using a week's

annual leave to stretch his paternity allowance to a luxurious three weeks, Chris returned to work. Then he was
back, re-familiarising himself with his three-hour daily
commute. 'Two weeks is not enough,' he concludes. 'Given
my role at work, it would not be feasible to have a significant amount of time off, but four weeks would have been
a better amount of time. I know my father didn't get any
paternity leave, so I suppose I feel lucky to have any. But it
can be a very difficult time for new parents to adjust; it is
essential that you're both there to make that adjustment.'

Andrew was back at work less than two weeks after an
agonising wait for a bed on the antenatal ward, eighteen
hours of labour, an induced birth, an aborted emergency
Caesarean and, finally, the arrival of a healthy baby boy.
Colleagues at his advertising firm were excited for him and
his new family right up to the 9.30 a.m. meeting. Then it
was back to normal. Except, as every parent before him has
also discovered, his 'normal' had changed for ever.

'Childbirth was even more traumatic than the films lead
you to believe,' he says. 'We were both shattered – her more
than me, of course – but then come the night feeds and the
whole puzzle of having a new and fragile non-speaking
entity living in your home, depending on you completely.
Until that point, life is chiefly about looking after yourself.
Now just brushing your own teeth seems a bit "me-me".'

Was two weeks long enough to make the adjustment?

'To be honest, I found looking after a young child far
more exhausting than going to work. It's only fair that the
load is shared, and firms should support that. If I'd had
a month, I could have supported my wife through a very

tough adjustment. I wouldn't want to take longer, though, because I'd worry about being usurped at work.'

There is a strong consensus among all the dads I interview: two weeks is not enough; a month would be great; any longer and they would start to worry that work couldn't cope without them. Or, whispered quietly in the paranoid small hours, that work might cope easily without them. This final worry makes sense if we're talking about special treatment for one man in a company where every other dad has stuck rigidly to the stiff-upper-lipped two-week limit. It would be brave to pioneer work–baby balance in a firm with a culture of presenteeism, and bravery is not a priority when you've just had a baby. But what would happen if the organisation decided to offer extended leave across the board? No need to be brave. Worry over. It might also address one of the root causes of inequality. Three out of four working mothers say they have experienced some kind of discrimination at work. More than half say pregnancy and maternity had a detrimental impact on their career. One in four bosses think it's fair to ask interviewees if they plan to have children and 40 per cent of mothers say they have been asked in interviews how motherhood might affect their work. Both these lines of enquiry are, by the way, illegal. They have been since 1975.

The inconvenient truth is that, despite increasingly robust iterations of the Equality Act, maternity leave costs firms much more than paternity leave. The situation the Equality Act is designed to police is not equal, so prejudice – whether overt or subconscious – is inevitable. This leaves working mums at a disadvantage and working dads trying to fulfil the role expected of them in the twenty-first century in a system that hasn't changed much since the nineteenth century.

So what, exactly, is expected of us? The idea that fathers should have significant involvement in the birth and early-years parenting of their children is still relatively new. Once again, some scholars have tried to argue that our moustachioed Victorian forebears were much more hands-on and much less disciplinarian than we tend to assume. Their evidence is not hugely convincing. In most Western countries, men were excluded from maternity wards until the 1960s and the actual delivery room until the 1970s. Becoming a father did not warrant a single day off work until even later. In the UK, paid paternity leave was only enshrined in law in 2003, and even then it was a token concession – a statutory £140 a week for up to two weeks.

Since then, things have changed dramatically. Such is the speed of the change that our exact role is still being defined. It is now almost unheard of – and very much frowned upon – for a father to be absent from the birth of his child, but some dads are exiled to the corridor by grumpy midwives, while others are up to their elbows in a birthing pool, Speedos on, scissors poised for the ceremonial umbilical snip.

A minority of experts have questioned whether the man's presence – in any capacity – is a good thing. Michel Odent, the renowned French obstetrician who has devoted his career to making childbirth easier for women, has long advocated that men should be kept as far from the labour ward as possible. 'The ideal birth environment involves no men in general,' he told the *Observer* a decade ago. 'Having been involved for more than fifty years in childbirths in homes and hospitals in France, England and Africa, the best environment I know for an easy birth is when there is nobody around the woman in labour apart from a silent, low-profile and experienced midwife ... no doctor and no husband, nobody else. In this situation, more often than not, the birth is easier and faster than what happens when there are other people around, especially male figures – husbands and doctors.' Odent argued that the mere presence of men increases the mother's tension and inhibits her production of the hormone oxytocin. 'If she can't release oxytocin, she can't have effective contractions, and everything becomes more difficult,' he said. 'Labour becomes longer, more painful and more difficult because the hormonal balance in the woman is disturbed by the environment that's not appropriate because of the presence of the man.' He blamed the rise in Caesareans in Britain on 'the masculinisation of the birth environment'.

Many of Odent's fellow obstetricians have taken issue with his conclusions. They argue that hospitalisation rather than masculinisation of birth causes most of the problems, and that dads actually perform a useful function by providing familiarity and support in an unfamiliar, stressful environment.

And so the debate continues. It is either very important that we are there or very important that we stay away. Which leaves us hovering by the door, waiting for cues from the midwife. The only certainty is that the trip to the pub to smoke cigars with your father-in-law to wait for white smoke from the hospital has been consigned to history.

The NCT even recommends that dads should help to write the birth plan. 'A birth plan can be great for helping to extract as much information from mum before the birth,' it advises on the dads' section of its website. 'She might not be at her most lucid when labour starts. It can also be empowering for dads.'

The shift in what is expected of fathers – and men in general – began towards the end of the last century. The rise of automation and globalisation meant that manufacturing jobs were disappearing. Conversely, the service sector was beginning to expand. Those traditional male attributes that would get you through a whole life down a coal mine were no longer required. In the 1970s, fewer than half of mothers in the UK worked. By the 1990s, that figure had risen to 60 per cent. By 2015, it had reached 75 per cent. As dual-income families became the norm rather than the exception, men had no option but to change with the times, too.

We can chart these changes through the various labels men have been given over the last four decades. The first of these – the New Man – arrived in the mid-1980s, just as it was becoming clear that gender roles were in flux. According to the *Oxford English Dictionary*, the New Man is 'someone who rejects sexist attitudes and the traditional male role, especially in the context of domestic responsibilities and childcare, and who is (or is held to be) caring, sensitive and non-aggressive'.

Acres of newspaper columns were devoted to exploring

this phenomenon, but it's hard to find any cast-iron evidence for the actual existence of this new species in the eighties. Certainly, the seventysomethings I've interviewed for this book don't recall being particularly 'new' when they were starting families. My father was present at my own traumatic birth in 1975 and only fainted when he stepped out for some fresh air afterwards, but he wouldn't describe himself as 'new'. He and many of his generation of dads claim they did more parenting and more housework than their fathers, but they all viewed the New Man moniker as a bit of a joke. A fad. It didn't help that the most famous New Man of all was Blu-Tacked to the bedroom walls of five million teenage girls. *L'Enfant* depicted a topless hunk cradling a baby and very quickly became Athena's best-selling poster, even outstripping the tennis girl with ants in her pants. This was the image that apparently represented the ideal man for young women of the time: ridiculously good looking, yes, but also totally on board with skin-to-skin parenting.

Of course, Athena dad was just a fantasy. In reality, the success of the poster turned Adam Perry, the model, into the exact opposite of a New Man. After Perry claimed that he had slept with three thousand women, *GQ* labelled him 'the world's most promiscuous man'. Shockingly, this did not make him any less appealing to women. 'Girls would just come up to me asking to be 3,001 or 3,002 and so on,' he told an interviewer. 'I was sleeping with different girls every day of the week. Sometimes two or three a day; a few times, two at a time or more.' The fact that a twenty-three-year-old took advantage of his fame is one thing. The fact that women continued to sleep with him after he admitted he was Not a New Man At All is quite another. What confusingly mixed signals. It's almost as if the women didn't care about his parenting skills. They were only interested in his six-pack. Naughty women.

Advertisers and retailers also had little interest in whether men were actually changing. They just wanted to sell stuff. And to do that, they did what they always do – they created and encouraged trends. The New Man – sensitive, caring and, most importantly, well groomed – was perfect for that. Women found him attractive, so men spent a fortune trying to be like him.

Although it's safe to say that the New Man was largely an invention of advertising execs and poster companies, he made enough of an impact to generate a backlash. In the 1990s, the rise of the New Lad was supposedly a reaction to feminism's 'shackling of men'. Enough with this tyrannical subjugation of our natural urges. We want to drink lager, watch football and not do any housework. Cue *FHM*, *Lock, Stock and Two Smoking Barrels* and *Men Behaving Badly*. And, of course, *Loaded* – the magazine 'for men who should know better'.

In his 2004 book *Cultures of Masculinity*, the sociologist Dr Tim Edwards concluded that both the New Man and the New Lad were 'intensely media driven ... they depend on, and are indeed constructed around, a series of commodity signifiers and consumerist practices, whether in the form of sharp suits and designer-label culture or classic cars and smoking ... In the final instance, it seems that they are niches in the market more than anything else, often defined according to an array of lifestyle accessories.'

When he wrote his book, Dr Edwards wouldn't have known that there were many more niches to come. The New Man and the New Lad were quickly followed by Metrosexual Man, Sensitive New Age Guy, Nice Guy and, most recently – and most stupidly – Spiritual New Age Guy, to sell, respectively, £50 haircuts, male moisturiser, 4×4 baby strollers and yoga classes. Nonsense niches, the lot of them, but underneath all the clumsy marketing, there was a genuine shift in attitudes.

In 1982, researchers found that 43 per cent of fathers had never changed a nappy. By 2000, the figure had fallen to just 3 per cent. Today, I doubt there is a father in the land who hasn't experienced that surge of panic, moments after you've removed the old nappy, moments before you've reached for the new nappy, when little Johnny grabs his knees, fixes you with a look of reddening determination and starts pushing again.*

A study by the University of London, published just in time for Father's Day 2014, reported that millennial dads spend seven times longer interacting with their children each day than their own fathers did with them forty years earlier. Now, before we all start handing out awards, it's worth noting that, in 1974, the average father's interaction with his kids amounted to a Rumpolian five minutes a day. By 2014, this had risen to just thirty-five minutes a day, compared to the average mother's one hour. Nevertheless, it's still a significant change, particularly when you consider that 1974

---

* Jacob Rees-Mogg and various septuagenarian rock stars excepted. I'm sure Boris Johnson is an expert in nappy origami.

dads didn't have to prise their kids away from their iPhones, Kindles and PlayStations or spend any of their quality time learning how a new Minecraft mod works. Back then, the only distractions were three television channels, the *Beano* and Pong.*

I took two weeks off when our first son was born fourteen years ago. Even though most of it was absorbed by an intricately planned home birth morphing into a fantastically unplanned emergency Caesarean, I still turned up at work the following Monday. There was no question of asking for more time off, even though Harriet couldn't lift Freddie, even though none of us had slept, even though I hadn't stopped to think how close I'd come to losing both of them – a thought that still troubles me all these years later. Why was there no question? It wasn't because my company or my boss were particularly unenlightened. It was partly because the entire culture of the company – and of almost every other company at the time – still required men to be men. The unspoken rule was very, very old school: we go back to work. The one concession from the previous generation to mine was that we could take two whole weeks of paternity leave. Any more than that was just an indulgence.

---

* I did have one argument about screen-time with my dad in 1983. I was eight and had spent the afternoon stuck on level eight of Chuckie Egg, a Spectrum 48k game in which you – Hen-House Harry – would climb ladders and jump across platforms collecting eggs while patrolling hens tried to eat you. Dad was in his midlife-crisis jogging phase and wanted to go for a run round the local park. I refused to accompany him. But, you know, it wasn't like I was weeing in a carrier bag to avoid taking a break from an all-consuming game. Unlike Fortnite, Chuckie Egg had a save function. It was also boring, but not quite as boring as going for a jog.

It was also partly because of me. I didn't consider asking for more time. It didn't even occur to me. I was now, suddenly, the sole provider. I would put work first because I was putting my family first. I wanted to show that I was still the same dependable employee. Fatherhood had made a world of difference but I wanted to prove that it had made no difference at all.

As you arrive in your thirties, you are, all being well, several rungs up the career ladder. You are earning more and you have some responsibility. At last! All the slogging away at school and university, all the tests, all the long hours on no salary and then a pitiful salary and then a slightly less pitiful salary are finally – finally – beginning to pay off. And it has to pay off because you now have dependants. It is more important than ever that you succeed or, as the little voice in your head whispers in the small hours, that you don't fail. And so you embark on your new double life. By day, you're the consummate professional, unchanged but for the occasional proud-dad video share ('Look – he smiled'). By night (and early in the morning and at the weekend), you're focused on trying not to kill this tiny, useless bundle of matter that has so recently made his terrifying, medieval, blood-soaked entrance into your world.

You used to wake up with more than enough time for a shower and maybe breakfast with your beloved. Now, you wake up seconds after you've just got back to sleep: 3 a.m., 4 a.m., then, irredeemably, 5.30. How many times can a man watch *In the Night Garden* before it's time to go to work? (Answer: five.) Total, unremitting exhaustion, the sort that makes terrorists give up the rest of their cell, and you're only the support act. You're not even bearing the brunt of it.

Back when life was simple, the rest of the cave dwellers would have helped. All the cavemen and cavewomen – the cavepeople? – would have clubbed together – literally – to raise a newborn infant. Now, we have to do it in our own individual family unit with, if we're lucky, the occasional reprieve from a benevolent aunt, brother or visiting granny. How did that happen? How have we regressed from where we were ten thousand years ago? Because, as expectations of fatherhood have changed, society has changed too. In the 1950s, homes faced on to the street. Children played football in that street. Doors were left unlocked. Everyone knew everyone else. It was all very Betjeman. By the 2000s, homes had turned away from the street to face their back gardens. Double-glazing companies made a killing with those fancy bi-fold doors to 'bring the outside in'. Between 2005 and 2015, the number of de-gardened front gardens tripled, and the craze for paving continues. The superficial reason is that we need somewhere to park our cars – residential zones be damned – but the underlying cause is far more tectonic.

Today, front gardens are for parking, not socialising. Back gardens are where the heart is. Community has contracted to a nuclear level. Yes, I know, that's a sweeping generalisation, but it's borne out by countless conversations I've had with the dads of today. The vast majority of us parent in relative isolation. The closest we get to a community are the other parents we meet in our parenting groups. All we have in common with each other is that we worked out how to get from slides one and two to slide three at approximately the same time. Such is our blind devotion to the cult of the individual that asking for help is seen, in the most damaging, patriarchal terms, as weakness. As we share war stories during our increasingly sporadic trips to the pub, we pride ourselves on our ability 'to manage' and no more.

In the past, the local community would rally around a new family, share and dissipate the chaos, relieve the psychological and emotional pressure. Now we do it all alone, behind closed doors, knowledge passed from unreliable internet forum to Google-panic dads rather than from a wise great aunt to the street's newest mum via the woman who runs the bakery. I would take my rose-tinted version of 1950s parenting, with its street cricket, its powdered eggs and its free babysitting, any day.

'When my firstborn arrived, I was working for someone who was very happy to remind anyone approaching parenthood that she had taken just four weeks off when she became a mother,' says Andreas, a healthcare executive, ironically enough. 'She wore it as a badge of pride. Every time I asked to leave early or take a couple of days, she would also remind me of my priorities. She wasn't overt about it, but I was under no illusion that taking time off to be a dad was a bit wet.'

Andreas ended up resigning but Pete, a sales executive, just buckled down and did what he was told. 'Our company was laying people off every quarter,' he says. 'Anyone who looked like they weren't prioritising work was out. So I took one week's paternity leave and threw the odd sickie when my wife was really struggling. There was absolutely no room to indulge any plan for a modern, participating father. It was easily the hardest period of my life and I wasn't even the one at home trying to raise a family.'

As many as one in four fathers suffers from postnatal depression – about the same as mothers – but it is still taboo to discuss the concept of male postnatal depression, let alone admit to it. There is an entirely understandable sense that men have it comparatively easy. We're not the ones giving birth. We have no idea. Men complaining about how hard a birth was for them is just a terrible, terrible look. But, as it stands, we are expected to participate in the birth, return to work like nothing happened, and then sustain our working lives while also being non-Victorian, hands-on fathers. Something has to break but something absolutely can't break now, not with all this new responsibility. So it goes inside, bottled up, and waits.

The evolutionary anthropologist Anna Machin argues that 'men are where women were in the 1980s: they are told, "You can have it all," then discover they can't without a considerable negative impact on their physical and mental wellbeing ... engendered by trying to juggle different elements of their life without any support.'

Things are beginning to change, though. Employers are beginning to cotton on to the idea that fathers are not only *expected* to be more hands-on but actually *want* to be. Several companies have recently upgraded their paternity-leave policies in recognition of this. In November 2017, for example, Aviva announced that its staff would be entitled to fifty-two weeks of parental leave, twenty-six of them on full pay, regardless of gender. In the first ten months of the new policy, two-thirds of the company's 228 male employees who took parental leave opted for the full six months of paid leave. Only a mad 5 per cent stuck resolutely to the traditional fortnight.

Be warned, fellow two-week dads. Talking to these Avivan frontierspeople can be quite galling. Take Peter, from one of the company's regional offices, who describes his first two weeks of fatherhood as 'a total blur': 'We weren't even in a routine, so it would have been very difficult for my wife if I'd gone back then. She had to have a Caesarean, so she wasn't allowed to drive for six weeks and getting around would have been a problem.'

Was six months too long, though?

'It was incredible having so much time to bond with my daughter, not missing any of those "firsts",' he says. 'I think it was the perfect amount of time. I had come into work for a few "keep in touch" days, so I wasn't totally out of the loop. Everyone was supportive and within a month it was as if I hadn't been away. Hopefully, in years to come, my experience won't be so unusual. People won't react with shock or surprise when a man says he's taking six months to care for his child. It will be considered as normal as a woman doing it.'

Iain, another Aviva employee who was sensible enough to take the full six months, is also incredulous at the idea of going back to work after just a fortnight. 'I honestly don't know how we would have coped,' he says. 'I don't think it was until around the six-week point that we all started to settle into a routine, until we could leave the house in less than an hour without forgetting anything, until we could enjoy being parents. Both of us being around meant that Charlie settled quicker and, in our opinion, started to develop at an earlier age. We would hear the stories of other parents having to get to grips with life having gone back to work at two weeks. It sounded impossible.'

When I ask Caroline Prendergast, Aviva's interim chief people officer (the non-interim one is on paternal leave), to describe the impact of the new policy, she is, as you would expect, full of enthusiasm. 'It gives our employees a chance to enjoy parenthood properly, but it also gives them a natural sabbatical,' she says. 'They come back refreshed and ready for work.' But what about the cost? Those two-hundred-plus men taking six months each: that's a century of salaries. 'We work in teams, so in most cases it's not a direct cost,' she says. 'If someone is away, the team can usually cover for them. The advantages – happy staff with a decent work–life balance – offset any costs.'

After a tense start to parenthood ('My daughter almost drowned in her own poo in the womb'), Charles agrees that his six months at home had a positive effect on his attitude to work. 'I actually found an increased appetite to work,' he says. 'It was like a new job and, of course, it had more meaning now I had to support a child.' On the other hand, he is the only Aviva employee who has anything even vaguely negative to say about the experience. 'My partner and I had never spent that much time with each other,' he admits. 'It caused a bit of friction, particularly given that we were both tired. But we worked through it.'

Richard, another employee, makes the point that while prospective parents tend to focus on the birth itself, the first few months of parenthood – when you're on your own – can be just as challenging. 'I know Victoria and Leni would have found a way to cope if I had gone back after two weeks,' he says. 'But, honestly, I don't know how people do it. Neither of us was prepared for the challenges of establishing breastfeeding, for example. Having me there for support gave Victoria the time to keep trying. The UK has one of the lowest rates of breastfeeding in the world, and I wouldn't be surprised if this was caused in part by new mothers not having the support around them at home. I'm also not surprised that many mothers experience postnatal depression. If Victoria had had to deal with the demands of a newborn baby in isolation, it would have been really tough.'

Aviva is not the only firm to make its parental-leave policy gender neutral. American Express, IBM and Twitter now offer twenty weeks' paternity leave on full pay, Spotify and Etsy six months, and all Netflix employees can take up to a year. But when Aviva asked Mumsnetters what they thought of the idea, the response was tellingly mixed. 'My husband would love to take this up if it was offered in his workplace, but he would find it hard to get it sanctioned by his managers,' said one. 'They thought he was odd for wanting two weeks for our first child.'

'In today's economic climate, six months is too long to be away from the workplace in career terms,' said another.

Perhaps the most conclusive comments came from a new mother who felt that equal parental leave would change people's opinions about the hiring of women. 'You may think this sort of discrimination doesn't happen any more, but my boss was open about how he wouldn't hire another woman in fertility,' she said. 'The last two went on maternity leave within two years of starting.'

When I mention Aviva's new policy to a friend, a father of three, he also remains unmoved by the case for balance. 'This country would grind to a halt if we all had that long off,' he says, reminding me, not for the first time, that he took only one week off to welcome each of his kids. The evidence suggests that he is wrong. The country would manage. With a rethink of how we tackle the Herculean task of parenthood, how we share it and how we would do better if we admitted we needed help, it might even thrive.

Perhaps there are lessons to be learnt from other countries. We could follow the Scandinavian model, where higher tax rates allow for huge investment in the welfare state. Both parents can work in the comforting knowledge that they have the support of a well-funded, high-quality, state-provided childcare programme. On a research trip to Stockholm, I found it almost impossible to find an employee who thought their work–life balance was anything other than wonderful. The dads work flexi-time; the mums work flexi-time. The office crèche is lovely. Everyone sits together at the table for dinner, which is fresh and healthy and not just meatballs. And Sweden has among the highest levels of work equality on the planet. Hurrah for the happy Swedes.

In the interests of making a cast-iron, bullet-proof argument, I should end this Swedish sojourn there. In the interests of full-disclosure, damn it, I have to point out that the Land of Volvo is not quite as utopian as it sounds. That cherished equality comes at the cost of actually raising the children. It might be properly funded childcare, but that still means someone else is doing the parenting of mini-Swedes from a very young age. And their much-lauded work–life balance is also questionable. In Stockholm's Epicenter – 'a house [deep breath] of digital innovation for digital scale-ups, corporates, intrapreneurs and entre-preneurs' – the whole ethos is about making work less work-like. It has a 'chief disruption officer' who encour-ages interaction between member companies 'because disruption is an important part of the innovation process'. Prospective members are vetted for niceness before they're allowed to join because Epicenter doesn't want any 'office nightmares'. It even has five-foot robots with iPads for faces so workers can wander virtually down the corridors and chat to colleagues from the comfort of their own homes. And absolutely everything – from the desks and chairs to the pot plants and lockers – is on wheels. This gives the intra/entrepreneurs the freedom to shape their working environment to suit their mood. 'The only thing here that is constant is change,' announces the guy who's giving me the tour, with such sincerity that I don't know whether to vomit or immediately move to Stockholm.

'It's not cool to say you work an eighty-hour week around here,' says one intrapreneur, shortly after telling me what an intrapreneur actually is. 'You work hard when you need to, but if you're here all the time, it means you've got the planning wrong.' He can work from home whenever he wants – no judgement from his colleagues – and if he has a meeting scheduled but it's his turn with the kids, he can always use one of the iPad robots. This flexibility is a key part of Stockholm's admirably revisionist approach to achieving the perfect work–life balance. Presenteeism is old-fashioned, inefficient, 'not cool'.

But when I press him, he admits that he can find it hard to switch off. He always has his phone with him, and he checks his emails 'constantly'. 'Last night, we were having dinner,' he says, a little sheepishly. 'I was using my phone, and my wife – who is an entrepreneur – was using hers. Our son told us to put the phones away.' That is quite something – an eleven-year-old boy telling his parents to get off their screens and engage.

My new intrapreneur friend, with his entrepreneur wife and his disapproving son, is not an outlier. The more flexible work becomes, the more it fits around our lives, the harder it is to escape. Technology inveigles itself into our homes under the pretext of making our lives easier and more convenient. In Chapter Seven, I'll examine the extent to which that is not the case. For now, I'm taking the Swedish version of working parenthood with a sizeable pinch of salt.

The German model is more patriarchal: dads predominantly work, mums predominantly stay at home (although a majority of the latter now work part-time). There is less equality in work but more actual parenting. German children start kindergarten when they turn three, but formal education only begins at the age of six. In 2007, Germany introduced shared parental leave of up to fourteen months to encourage fathers to take a more active role in raising their kids and by 2017, one in three German fathers was taking two months of paternity leave.

When the economist Marcus Tamm examined the effects of this new policy, he found that the more time men took off immediately after the birth, the more time they spent parenting once they had returned to work. It was not a small effect. Dads who took two months' paternity leave went on to spend an hour and a half more with their children each day than dads who took a fortnight or less. (They also did an extra hour of housework each day.) Clearly and obviously, if a father takes the time to establish a bond in the very early days, that bond endures.

In the UK, we appear to be aiming for a budget version of the apparently progressive Scandinavian model rather than the apparently archaic German one. Childcare provision was a key battleground in the run-up to the 2019 general election. Each of the three main parties in England claimed it was the most visionary when it came to the issue of women in work. The Conservatives pledged a billion pounds of investment in childcare centres. 'Raising a family should be the most fulfilling experience of your life,' declared their manifesto. 'But for too many parents, the cost of childcare is a heavy burden.' What a great non-sequitur. Labour pledged thirty hours of free childcare a week for all of the nation's two-, three- and four-year-olds. The Liberal Democrats promised thirty-five hours a week from nine months, as long as both parents were in work. 'Parents wanting to go back to work will get the help they need, knowing that their child will be happy, healthy and ready to start school,' they claimed.

So, under the pretext of 'helping mothers get back to work', politicians of all hues appear determined to make raising children a responsibility of the state. Daring to question that approach runs the risk of being labelled patriarchal. But let's take that risk.

In a society where, by and large, men work and women raise children, equality campaigners are sure to argue that men end up running the show. It is vital, they say, that women are represented in boardrooms, in rooms where the big decisions are made, in the upper echelons – and every other echelon – of government. Only a fool or a time-travelling Victorian would disagree. Look at how the twentieth century – and all the other ones – went. It is indisputable that we need more female power in the twenty-first.

But moving towards a society where we have total equality in the workplace to the absolute detriment of our children doesn't seem sensible either. None of the fathers I've interviewed like the idea of sticking their pre-toddlers in state-(under)funded, poor-quality childcare for thirty-five hours each week. They would rather be fathers.

As it stands, the majority of men are trying to be hands-on fathers without risking their crucial role as providers. They are working and then they are parenting and then they are working again. The transition from one to the other is lightning fast, like a knackered Clark Kent in a phone box. Rather than sacrificing work time in order to create more parent time, they just give up everything they used to enjoy before they became fathers. Friends, hobbies, sport, baths, sleep – all gone. Their lives become two-dimensional.

What is the answer? How do we square the need for equality with the need to raise our children? Well, we could swap. We could all become stay-at-home dads. I know several men who raise their children while their partners work, and, despite some teething issues around ego and status, they seem relatively happy. But working mums in single-income households have the same problems with balance as working dads in single-income households. So we need a more sustainable solution. When I'm feeling optimistic, I think we might just be fumbling our way towards it.

Step one: we re-evaluate what it means to go on maternity (and paternity) leave. If a mother takes a year ... or two ... or four out to raise her young children, employers should acknowledge that she has not sidelined her career but broadened her skill set. Because, obviously, she has. Raising a child is far tougher than any team-bonding nonsense in the Brecon Beacons. Building a raft out of four oil drums and some rope is a piece of cake compared to installing a car seat on two hours' sleep while a toddler is screaming in your ear. Negotiating a new sales contract is nothing – absolutely nothing – compared to securing a peaceful resolution to an iPad stand-off. New mums must find new reserves of patience, endurance, strength, balance, determination and more patience while reading *Each Peach Pear Plum* seventy-three times a day. As and when they do choose to return to work, that should count for something. Celebrate them. Utilise them. Promote them.

But dads want – and are expected – to play a hands-on role, too. This has changed in a generation, and it continues to change now. A music teacher tells me hardly any dads turned up when she started a class for parents and toddlers ten years ago. Now it's close to fifty–fifty. Ten years ago, one of the few dads felt patronised by some of the mums: 'They kept making suggestions about feeds and nappies,' he says. 'It was as if they thought I didn't know what I was doing.' According to the teacher, that doesn't happen any more. Dads are expected to cope and they do. But this change has happened, and is still happening, without society in general acknowledging the fact. Society frowns if you don't attend the birth of your kid, but it also frowns if you ask for a reasonable amount of parental leave. So . . .

Step two: a minimum of two months' paid paternity leave. This will give new dads the time they need to form that vital bond with their kids. The time they need to process what's just happened. It's good for the family and it's good for the whole of society. The cost to the NHS of all the physical and mental health problems that have their genesis in early-years development is unquantifiable, but it's certainly high. If we invest in healthy, stable starts for our children, we'll all benefit. And a paternity 'break' is beneficial for employers and employees, too. Men are expected to work from the moment they leave education to the day they retire. Forty years and counting of pushing the boulder up the hill. I'm not suggesting that raising an infant is easy, but at least it's different. A change – even if that change is as terrifying as parenthood – is as good as a rest. If the dads at Aviva are anything to go by, a man who returns to work after months rather than weeks will be glad to be back, raring to go, renewed. Ready to have another go at the boulder.

Step three: the return of the single-income family. Whoa! Hold on. Put the pitchfork away. I'm not talking about the old-school, unequal, working-man, housewife-woman single-income family.* I mean a new variation where both parents work part time: a two-job, one-income family. Or two jobs and one and a third incomes. Or one and a half. The idea is that both parents work flexibly while the kids are young. Three-day weeks, four-day weeks, nine-day fortnights, a bit of childcare when it's needed ... In short, whatever works, whatever pays the mortgage, whatever maintains a healthy work–life balance, whatever allows parents to be parents. (But only if that's what you want. In my utopian society, the state won't force parents to be hands-on. It just won't penalise them if they want to be.)

Now, I admit that this will require a few minor tweaks and gentle adjustments. First, there will have to be a massive house-price crash. House-price rises have been outpacing pay increases for decades – what a great, insidious way to ramp up the pressure on families. Second, we'll have to accept that the 'two-income trap' is a reality and introduce measures to avoid it. Coined by Harvard law professor (and now Massachusetts senator) Elizabeth Warren in 2004, the 'two-income trap' refers to the pressure families endure when both parents are in full-time work. In theory, such families should be more equal and have more resources than single-income households. In practice, Warren argued, the second earner's income is

---

* My grandparents had an old-fashioned set-up. He worked, she raised the children. Not surprising, because this was the 1950s. But my grandmother, God rest her soul, had her patriarchal limits. One evening, my grandfather, God rest his soul, complained that his tea was late when he got in from work. The following day, Granny was waiting at the bus stop. As he and all his work colleagues disembarked, she handed him a plate of food. 'There's your tea,' she said. 'Not late today, I hope.' He didn't complain again.

often negated by higher childcare fees, commuting costs and house prices.

Moreover, the traditional two-parent, one-earner family had options in a crisis. 'If her husband was laid off, fired, or otherwise left without a paycheck,' wrote Warren, 'the stay-at-home mother didn't simply stand helplessly on the sidelines as her family toppled off an economic cliff; she looked for a job to make up some of that lost income ... A stay-at-home mother served as the family's ultimate insurance against unemployment or disability – insurance that had a very real economic value even when it wasn't drawn on.' Modern two-income families have none of this adaptability. No safety net.

We'll return to the close and destructive relationship between money and success in Chapter Eight, but for now we just need to focus on one simple (and annoying) rule: stretching ourselves to the point where both parents have to work full-time, all the time, is a bad idea.

Yes, I know. I sound like a wand-waving socialist with Diane Abbott's grasp of economics. But we've already reached the point where middle-aged men are hiding in baths, collapsing in boardrooms and still working five days a week with potentially fatal heart conditions. Something has to give. Some sacrifices have to be made. Our obsession with (what we perceive to be) success is unhealthy. Our priorities need to change in the same way as our expectations of fatherhood already have. For a period of time when the children are young, we need to create some space. We need to demand flexibility from government, industry ... and ourselves. As it stands, the burden still falls on working mothers to negotiate part-time hours or job shares. Working fathers need to start sharing that burden. As parenting becomes less patriarchal, work should too.

The American psychologist Allan Schore has devoted much of his career to studying parent–child relationships. He was one of the first to notice and describe the profound effect of neglect and attachment trauma on a child's neurological development. And, because boys develop at a different rate to girls, this effect varies with gender. 'The maturation of the male right brain is more protracted,' he tells me. 'It is therefore more immature and vulnerable than the female right brain. In a secure attachment, the mother offers affect regulation over this period of vulnerability. Not so in insecure relationships, especially in histories of attachment trauma and neglect, to which boys are more vulnerable than girls.

'The key to the infant's attachment is associated with access to an adult right hemisphere, which usually is more developed in females. That said, of course men have right hemispheres too, and so the father's tenderness and love can act as a secondary source of regulation, even in the first year. In the second year, when the left hemisphere comes into a growth spurt, the father directly shapes that development.'

Ideally, the right and left hemispheres should balance. Too little of the former and too much of the latter, and you risk 'narcissistic personality disorders, poor social intelligence, and chronic problems with intimacy and empathy', warns Schore. In related news, Donald Trump's mother was frequently absent in his first few years of life, while his father reportedly ruled the house like a tyrant. It is hardly controversial to suggest that the real-estate developer Frederick Christ Trump's approach to parenting failed to provide the levels of tenderness and love that would have provided a much-needed secondary source of regulation for his son. And look how that turned out.

Even in optimal circumstances, boys' brains develop at a slower rate than girls', but dads can play an important role in nurturing that development from the very beginning. This is exciting and empowering. Although the film industry is still churning out new iterations of *Three Men and a Baby* – 'Aren't men useless? Haha. Look, that guy can't even change a nappy'* – today's dads are moving away from the stereotype. We have a role. We are not weak if we accept it.

---

* Last Christmas, *The Times'* critic awarded one star to *Playing with Fire*, a film in which a firefighter struggles to look after a baby. '*Three Men and a Baby*, but worse,' he concluded, witheringly. The poor characterisation of men I detailed in Chapter Three is magnified when they have children to raise. Homer Simpson, Raymond from *Everybody Loves Raymond*, Fred Flintstone, every dad in every nappy commercial, Hugh Dennis's Pete in *Outnumbered* and Lee Mack's Lee Mack in *Not Going Out* are all incompetent, but the one that really gets my goat is Daddy Pig, Peppa's obese, amnesiac father. Teaching kids that dads are deadbeats, one toddler at a time.

CHAPTER FIVE

Men and exercise

S o, here we are in the middle. You've conformed to society's requirements. You've passed the tests, climbed the ladders and avoided the snakes. After four or five decades of slogging away, pleasing teachers, then bosses, you've reached the point where you can say you're a proper grown-up with some – or maybe all – of the trappings of success: a (heavily mortgaged) house, a decent car (on finance), a loving partner, maybe a family, possibly one of those curved televisions. Whatever it is, you've got it and you've done it. You were encouraged to be successful in work and life and you've done exactly what was expected of you. Congratulations.

On the surface, it might seem strange that this is exactly when so many men don't feel like celebrating. But when you think about it, it's not strange at all. You're on the summit of the mountain. You've made it. Now what have you got to look forward to aside from trudging back down again? Everyone knows that climbing down the mountain is the dangerous bit. That's when people fall down crevasses. Great.

The author Paolo Gallo was not far off the summit when, to stretch the metaphor badly, his wife staged something of a mountain rescue. He was forty-five when he took her out to a posh restaurant to celebrate their tenth wedding anniversary. There was a cake, but before he could enjoy it, his wife cut it in two and put one half in the bin. 'Because we're only celebrating our fifth anniversary,' she told him.

'No, our tenth,' said Gallo.

'No, our fifth. Because you've been away travelling for five of those ten years. And I won't be here in another ten years if you carry on this way.' Brutal.

At the time, Gallo was a director at the World Bank in Washington. On the surface, then, a success, a big shot. But his remit covered eighty countries and he was away, on average, for 188 days each year. The cake was the last of several increasingly obvious red flags. Another had come while he was having lunch with a colleague. Their boss called to unload a list of demands and, when he rang off, Gallo's colleague said, 'That guy will be the death of me.' Two weeks later, he dropped dead. He was fifty-five.

Twelve years on, Gallo no longer spends 188 days a year flying from one country to the next. At the end of his transition to happiness, he wrote *The Compass and the Radar: The Art of Building a Rewarding Career while Remaining True to Yourself.* His book had the potential and, let's be honest, the title, to join the creaking shelf of unhelpful self-help guides, but for one impressive detail: Gallo really did trade 'success' for a more rewarding way to live.

He believes the crisis that engulfs so many fortysomething workers is inevitable. 'You spend the first twenty years of your career running, running, running,' he says. 'You reach a point where you question whether you can keep running like this for another twenty years.' There are two classic responses. The first is what he describes as 'German soldier syndrome' – head down, keep marching. 'A fast track to burnout.' The second is to buy a sports car, get divorced and find a younger model, 'which only provides more complication – financial and emotional'.

Gallo's solution is to address the inevitable crisis before you reach full implosion. 'Be mindful of the price that you pay, and you make other people pay, for your career,' he says. 'Reconnect with what is meaningful in your life, which is never usually about power or money. Then ask yourself what you stand for, what is important to you and what are your values.' From this process, he assures me, you will start to have ideas about what to do next.

For Gallo himself, his wife's cake-based ultimatum sent him on a five-year transition out of the upper echelons of the financial world. He swapped his Mercedes for a second-hand Honda Civic, reduced other outgoings and saved enough money to go back to school for a year. Today, he is a teacher, a life coach, an author and, first and foremost, a father. 'I earn seventy per cent less now, but the things I do now bring me joy,' he says.

'I've learnt that expecting the solution to your problems to come from others is not going to work,' he says. 'There will always be a jerk disturbing you on Christmas Day. Remember that the highest concentration of psychopaths is in prison, but the second highest is made up of CEOs and senior managers.'

I think Gallo was lucky. He had that defining, cake-based moment of clarity – and he then had the bravery and resolution to act upon it. Most of the men I've interviewed are, understandably, more risk-averse. Instead of a wife and a cake, they have the little voice inside their head muttering about the futility of life. That little voice has always been relatively easy to block out. There have always been more pressing issues. School was one test after another. Early adulthood was motivation by deficiency. Then kids arrived and they had little voices of their own. Now, in midlife, it's no longer obvious what has to be done and what must come next. You have to think about it and that's the last thing you want to do.

'I don't want to think about it.'

'I don't want to dwell on my own happiness ... or lack of it. I worry I might not be able to get out of bed in the morning.'

'Can we change the subject?'

And on and on and on.

Rather than follow Gallo's advice and take several years to plan and implement a happier future, many men go for a cunning variation on the German soldier syndrome. They find a hobby, a new sport, a minor administrative role in the local am-dram society. Anything to keep

busy. Anything to block out that treacherous, whisper-
ing Gollum. That was certainly my first strategy. Like a
million middle-aged men before me and a million after,
I decided that the best way to prove that I wasn't getting
old was to pursue hitherto unprecedented levels of physical fitness.

Things I have tried to postpone the acceptance of my own ephemerality

1. Surfing

Classic midlife behaviour. Not long after my fortieth
birthday, I drove to Croyde, surf capital of north Devon,
with several forty/fifty-something friends, determined to
catch a wave on an actual surfboard rather than the kids'
body board I'd been using since the 1990s. I had watched
all of the YouTube tutorials and bought all of the gear.
I was ready. Manfully, I strode out through the autumn
squall, very much like the man from that Guinness ad.
And then Max, whose decision to go for a peroxide blond
Mohican had coincided neatly with his arrival in midlife,
turned to me and said, 'You've got your wetsuit on back
to front.'

2. Cycling

It worked for one forty-five-year-old marketing manager
from Surrey, who told the *Guardian* that becoming a

Middle-Aged Man In Lycra transformed his life. 'I found myself out of breath kicking a football around the garden with my son and thought, do I really want to be an overweight dad who can't keep up with his kids?' he explained. 'Within three months I was hooked – and, yes, I splashed the cash on the gear. I do occasionally cycle with a friend because it's nice to catch up, but I mainly do it by myself and it's like a complete decompression time that does me the world of good. I can work out everything while on my bike – work stuff, issues that are bothering me. It's a great way of meditating on life.'

I'm happy for him, but it didn't work for me. I bought the mountain bike and the Swiss, tissue-wrapped Lycra and I cycled every weekend for four years. When I rode on my own, I got bored. No decompression. No working out anything. When I rode with friends, I got left behind. Or we just spent the whole time grumbling about work. The second time I was wing-mirrored into a hedge, I decided to let the cars win. Running would be more relaxing.

3. Running

Running wasn't more relaxing. I blame the app. I downloaded it innocently enough and went for my usual run. When I finished, it congratulated me on being in the top seventy-six per cent of runners on that route. That's deceptive phraseology, isn't it? A more honest approach would have been: 'Unlucky, mate. You're in the bottom twenty-four per cent.' The app's attempt to look on the bright side made it worse. What was going on? I was fit ... relatively ...

for my age. I did not, as far as I knew, have type-2 diabetes. I was not morbidly obese. How could I be down there with the chain-smoking, triple-chinned, sofa-dwelling 24 per centers?

The following day, I ran again and made it into the top three-quarters. Then, after a few more attempts, the top two-thirds. Then, coughing up small pieces of lung, the top half. The app was full of praise. I was awarded all sorts of entirely spurious achievement badges, which my ego received like it was on an Olympic podium. The next week, my time did not improve. Crestfallen. The week after that, same again. Then my knees went.

4. Letting myself go

When some people discover they have a year to live, they abandon everything they don't love and fill their days with bucket-list adventures. Given how quickly life – and in particular midlife – passes, it's puzzling that the rest of us don't do this, too.

'Live every day like your hair's on fire,' read the poster in the surf café we holed up in after I'd worked out that surfing wasn't for me. We all laughed our cynical middle-aged laughs at that typically brainless example of positive thinking. Imagine living every day with your hair on fire. Just one day would be fairly intolerable. But every ... single ... day? You'd never get anything done.

Since then, I've tried to address and eliminate that cynicism. It's a defence mechanism deployed to avoid talking about what's really going on. The poster was stupid, but the sentiment was spot on. Why waste time doing things you don't love?

I didn't go hot-air ballooning or heli-skiing or skydiving or any of the obvious things you'd do if the doctor had given you bad news or your hair was on fire. I just decided to let myself go. With four decades left if I'm lucky, two decent ones if I'm not, why would I spend any of it jogging? Trainers back in the loft. App deleted. Ironing shirts? Gone. Clothes shopping? Gone too. I replaced gym sessions and a moderately high level of personal grooming with alcohol and not giving a shit what I looked like. I shaved every fortnight rather than every day. I abandoned breakfast – a meal I've never liked. I stopped going to parties (which are always awful) and lunches (which are just static, condensed versions of parties followed by work rather than sleep). Instead, I lived the life and ate the diet of a self-indulgent, self-pitying hermit. In other words, the hair-on-fire poster's target audience.

5. Not letting myself go

It turns out that it doesn't take long for people to stop inviting you to things if you always say no. I didn't particularly mind being a social pariah but drinking on your own has its limits in that, very quickly, it doesn't. Faced with a total lack of exercise, a wilfully poor diet and whisky, my body began to revolt. There were sharp pains, dull aches, numb bits, tingling bobs and other symptoms it didn't pay to google. After six months of concerted hair-on-fire inertia, the preceding thirty-plus years of relatively healthy living and regular exercise counted for nothing. Standing, breathless, at the top of a very gentle hill, I accepted what I knew already: the not-giving-a-shit plan did not have the legs.

I stopped drinking in January 2019. For four weeks, it was all a bit *Trainspotting*. The other Dry Januaryers were celebrating the joys of sobriety: 'I've got so much extra time' ... 'I simply love the mornings' ... 'I've taken up knitting/origami/cross-stitch/hang-gliding.'

I just felt awful. Nauseous. Exhausted. Bored. Permanently hungover.

It took until the end of February before I began to feel better. I started exercising again. I started telling all the flaky Wet Februaryers how much I simply loved the mornings. One newly lengthened evening ('No, I've got so much extra time'), Harriet and I took Marie Kondo's *The Life-Changing Magic of Tidying* to heart and threw out most of our shoes. The next evening, we did the same with our clothes. By the end of the week, the house had been transformed from the kind of cluttered mess you see on Channel 5's *Hoarders: Landfill in My Living Room* to a place that a mysophobic minimalist would find a bit much.

Of all the attempts to distract myself from the ephemerality of my own existence (and I haven't even mentioned obstacle-racing, learning the trumpet or that time I tried Mexican wrestling), this one, the boring, healthy, teetotal one has been the happiest. Despite a four-month bender late last year and several lapses during lockdown, it continues to this day.

*

Fitness is important. If you're fit, life is easier. You have more energy. You sleep better. You are less likely to drop dead, because lack of exercise is the second-biggest killer of middle-aged men after smoking. It's all really simple, route-one stuff.

But there's fitness and then there are the fitness obsessives. Men like the marketing manager from Surrey who go for a thirty-mile bike ride before breakfast, own more Lycra than underwear, and run ultra-marathons because marathons are too short. Their moods live and die by the current stats on their running apps. I am friends with some of these people. They pop round for tea ('Have you got herbal?') with their rictus grins and their heavily strapped knees. 'I'm training for the Iron Man. It's a real killer. I love it.'

But after the runner's high comes the runner's low. They're all bright-eyed and bushy-tailed as they build up to the next insane challenge they've carved out for themselves. But once the glow of achievement has faded, they're miserable, scrolling phones for the next, bigger fix. It's their way of proving they're not getting old. It's denial in Reeboks. It is – ironically – unhealthy.

The solution is not to take to the sofa, feed the pot belly, drink yourself to sleep and wait for the Grim Reaper to come knocking. You can still release the endorphins; you just have to do it without a stopwatch. Go for a run because you want to, not because you have a time to beat. Go for a cycle because it's a lovely day, not because you want to unleash your office-incubated aggression on a couple of horse-riders and an old lady crossing the road too slowly. To which my friends – doing muscle stretches in my kitchen – say, 'I couldn't do it if I didn't have a target.' To which I say, 'But that's the unsustainable bit. It's why Jonny Wilkinson got depressed after making that World Cup-winning drop goal. It's why James Cracknell should never have become the oldest rower in the Boat Race.'

As I've repeatedly said, this is not a self-help book but I am being helpful now. I've spent enough time faffing around with exercise fads to know.

If you treat exercise as a challenge to be met, then you're falling into the same trap that got us all into the midlife maelstrom in the first place. Life is full of targets, goals, ambitions and boxes awaiting their ticks. Our relentless pursuit of external validation, our need to compete and succeed, is unsustainable.

Ben Sinclair runs a health clinic in the Midlands. I'll introduce him properly in the next chapter but for now you just need to know that he spends his working days trying to convince his patients to live healthier lives. For a while, he didn't follow his own advice, which led to the familiar creep towards midlife misery. Fortunately, his day job meant he recognised the signs, so he prescribed two simple treatments. First, he started running through a forest. It's not a long run. He doesn't time it or log it on an app or compare himself to other runners on the same route. But it is a proper forest – wild and beautiful and 'when I run through it, I appreciate it,' he says. 'It brings me alive. And if I see a deer, I am sustained for the whole day. Men have a deep-seated need for adventure and part of what's killing us in the modern Western tradition is that we no longer have any adventure in our lives. We are sold a car on the basis that it can drive across the savannah, but we're only ever going to drive it to the supermarket. Where's the freedom?'

It's a good point. Men – sweeping generalisation klaxon – have a tendency to go to extremes with new projects. We buy all the gear, we set big, manly goals, we fail to meet those goals, and we sell all the gear on eBay. Our expectations are too high and, when the reality doesn't measure up, the whole lot goes in the bin. The idea that you can find freedom and adventure in a fifteen-minute trot through the forest at the end of the road is inspiring – and no one has to buy a one-way ticket to Alaska. Sinclair runs through the forest for the simple joy of running through a forest.

His second treatment is even more radical, but I think you're ready for it. At the end of each working day, he boards the train home and – brace yourself – switches off his smartphone. 'I made the conscious decision to do something on the commute that would help my mental state,' he says. During his phone-free journey, his focus is on contentment, something too many of us neglect. 'Through reflection, you can find contentment,' he says.

I know that sounds wishy-washy, but I've tried it and it works. You make a list – an actual list with a pen and paper – of all the things you're grateful for, including the people you love. You can even go through a meditation during which you declare your love for everyone you care for in your life. (The meditation can be whispered – we don't want to frighten your fellow commuters.)

'It's not very blokey,' Sinclair says, 'but I find it therapeutic. It means, hopefully, that you're not going to be a git to your wife when you get in. You're not carrying all the stresses of the day back home with you. You made time for reflection. You've reminded yourself of good things. You've got something left in the tank.'

You may think this is all a bit much, but just try it the next time you're nose-deep in a fellow commuter's armpit on a late-running service due to the late running of an earlier service. The change is incremental, and you might want to save the 'I love my wife/dad/postman' chant with accompanying finger cymbals until you're a pro and/or arrested. But do try it.

Delete MapMyRun, run through the forest or the wood or the park at your own pace, and make gratitude lists on the train or the bus or the escalator. Think of this as the first step in Paolo Gallo's pre-emptive strike against midlife misery. Don't wait for your wife to slice your anniversary cake in half. Start examining what makes you happy. It might be a short list. And things that don't make you happy might even try to crash the party. One of them might be the idea of writing gratitude lists, which would be very unhelpful of it. But it's all about mindset.

The psychotherapist Viktor Frankl was deported from Vienna to the Theresienstadt ghetto in Czechoslovakia in 1942. Two years later, he and his family were transported to Auschwitz. He survived but his wife and his parents were killed. When he returned to Vienna, he wrote *Man's Search for Meaning*, a remarkably hopeful, inspirational work based on his unimaginably horrific experiences. The meaning of life, he concluded, is found in every moment of living: 'Everything can be taken from a man but one thing:

the last of the human freedoms – to choose one's attitude in any given set of circumstances.'

So, write your gratitude list. It doesn't matter how short it is or how inconsequential some of the entries may seem. It's not like anyone else on the train will notice or care. They're all too busy answering supposedly urgent emails from people they definitely wouldn't put on their gratitude list.

CHAPTER SIX

Men and health

'My husband was proud to say that, in a career of more than twenty-five years, he had never taken a sick day,' began the letter from the worried wife. 'He has always been stressed but lately, that stress has become more acute. He works very long hours – he is always at his desk at seven in the morning and by the time he gets home, he is exhausted. We used to enjoy a very active sex life but now he's too tired. And last month, he started to get chest pains.'

The worried wife did what any worried wife would do when her husband starts complaining of chest pains. She urged him to go to the doctor. When it became clear that he wasn't going to break his twenty-five-year attendance streak for something as trivial as chest pains – this man has clearly never consulted Dr Google – she got tough with him. 'There are no attendance prizes in the cemetery, darling,' she told him. More obfuscation. So, in the great tradition of women trying to persuade men to accept the blindingly obvious without denting their pride, she adopted guerrilla tactics. She started leaving pertinent articles around the house. One of them happened to be a piece I'd written about how and why some men neglect their physical and mental health.

In the article, I'd written that it's not manly to admit you're struggling. In fact, it's taboo. Thanks to our patriarchal upbringing – 'big boys don't cry' – we're inclined to ignore aches, pains, lumps, bumps, nodules, flaps and mysterious swellings until someone hands us a carriage clock and/or we drop dead. Which comes first is secondary to reaching either conclusion with the minimum of fuss.

The husband read the article, perhaps clutching his chest as he did so, and took reluctant action. He made an appointment with his doctor. The doctor convinced him to see a psychotherapist, presumably to discuss stress but also to address his ambivalence towards his own health. 'Oh, and he's having emergency heart surgery next week,' the wife post-scripted.

I wrote back to agree, rather toadishly, that all men are ridiculous and expressed the hope that the surgery went well.

'Yes, a success,' came the reply a few days later. 'He took a whole week off work and I sent him to a spa just to make sure he rests. I'll keep you updated on the therapy.'

Even after surgery, this man's wife – who obviously loves him and would rather he didn't die – had to commit him to a health facility to ensure that he didn't head straight back to work. And I'm quite sure she spent that whole week fretting that her husband would stage a breakout and she would receive a phone call telling her he was last seen running towards his office in a back-to-front massage gown.

On the surface, it's madness. What was the fool thinking? Why did it fall to his wife to force him to be sensible? But this ignores the powerful forces at work on this man and so many others. A very large clue comes in the first sentence of her letter. He was proud ... and that pride was based on his unstinting commitment to work. Twenty-five years! In his mind, it was this that made him a successful man. If he couldn't work, then he was a failure and he could no longer be proud. The flip side of pride is shame; and shame, he no doubt figured, is worse than anything that might be causing chest pains. It was irrelevant that his employers would have understood. Or that his friends and family would have rallied around. It was how he felt about himself that mattered.

From the moment this man was first given a sweet or a sticker or a ruffle of his hair for being a good toddler, he has been trained – as we all are – to associate success, winning, good grades, good attendance, all that jazz, with happiness. Throughout his education and his career, this association grew even stronger, eventually eclipsing all else, even the inescapable fact that we are mortal and that he might need to see a doctor. By the time he had been working for twenty-five years without a break, associating all his self-worth with his job and his stoic, dependable, never-failed-us-yet presenteeism, it was inevitable that he had to be spa-sectioned to keep him away from his desk.

This is a chapter about health and how men tend to neglect it out of some misplaced sense of manliness. Yesterday morning, I was composing my latest little gratitude list on the train. It began, 'I am grateful we ignored all the warnings and adopted a Border collie that requires three long walks a day.' Yesterday evening, I was on one of those walks I'm so grateful for when I tripped and fell. Once I'd found the torch function on the phone I should have left behind (see Chapter Seven), I saw that the intense shooting pain was coming from the base of my thumb, which I'd impaled on a sharp branch on my way down. The javelin tip of the branch had travelled just over an inch up through the meat of my palm, so I think you'll agree I was brave to pull it out and even braver to stop the arcing fountain of blood with a heavy compress (my jacket). After a mile-long stagger home, I sopranoed for help (less brave) and my wife spent the next few minutes trying to clean the forest detritus from the wound without barfing.

'Maybe you should go to A & E?' she suggested.

'I'm fine ... and it's Saturday night.' (Knowing wink to the parents out there.)

'Okay. You can go tomorrow then.'

Tomorrow is now today. And because I've already researched this chapter, I decided it was okay to ask for help and took myself off to the minor injuries unit this morning. Bravely – again – I did not cry as the nurse scraped out the more deeply embedded woodland flora. I gasped a lot though, so she gave me a local anaesthetic. Which really, really hurt.

Still didn't cry. Apologised, actually, for wasting her time.

'I can't tell you how many men start by saying they wouldn't have bothered me, but their wife insisted,' said the nurse.

I have to go back tomorrow for an X-ray.

My correspondent's husband is by no means an outlier. A few years ago, a large study of census data concluded that women were more likely than men to say they were in poor health, but less likely to die over the following five years. In a more recent survey of men conducted by Bupa, 80 per cent of the respondents said it was 'the norm' for them to endure an illness rather than seek help from a medical professional. Almost half had let symptoms progress to the point where pain was 'unbearable' before conceding they might need help. Almost a third had let their mystery ailment linger for more than three weeks. Heroic ... or pointless and potentially dangerous? If the mystery ailment turns out to be serious, the lingering strategy is not what the unconsulted doctor would have ordered.

Bill Turnbull, the former *BBC Breakfast* presenter, was diagnosed with prostate cancer at the end of 2017. Two years later, in an interview with *The Times*, he admitted that he had been having aches, pains and bladder issues for months. He had dealt with these symptoms by taking painkillers and visiting an osteopath. It was only when his son saw him stumbling around the house one morning and urged him to see his GP that he finally booked an appointment.

'Typical man, I didn't want to hang around at the surgery,' said Turnbull. 'I didn't want to waste the GP's time. Would it have made a difference if I had? I don't know. It is very ironic that I'd been doing *Celebrity Great British Bake Off* in aid of cancer research and, unbeknown to me, I had it even then.'

In April 2018, the former Conservative health secretary Andrew Lansley, who helped launch a screening programme for bowel cancer, revealed that he was in stage three of the disease. He claimed his own party's failure to roll out the programme nationally had prevented an earlier diagnosis, but he still felt lucky, 'because I went to see my GP (after much nagging* from my wife) ... with spreading back pain, without any thought that it could be cancer.' Again, a man prevaricates. Again, a concerned wife talks sense.

In a snap survey conducted in a supermarket car park, I collar the first ten men who aren't quick enough to escape from a man with a clipboard and ask when they last went for a routine check-up. Two of them have been seen in the last year, but only 'because I had to for work'. Seven can't remember ... and are quite pleased that they can't. The tenth has made it to forty-seven without a single medical skirmish. No check-ups, no screenings, not even a reluctant

---

* The word 'nagging' crops up a lot when husbands talk about their wives, but never the other way round. It's a defensive code word for 'we're only doing what we're doing, seeking help, admitting weakness, getting tested for cancer, because our wives told us to, not because we're in any way unmanly'. Characterising a woman's concern as nagging is not only a classic example of everyday sexism; it also betrays misguided pride in our own obduracy. Our emotional immaturity is ingrained in our language. We blame – rather than thank – the people who persuade us to seek potentially life-saving help. Ridiculous.

capitulation after a prolonged bout of man flu. Nothing. 'I'm fitter than I've ever been,' he says, affecting an ironic body-builder pose.

'He's not,' interrupts his wife.

'I am,' he insists. 'I cycle a hundred miles a week.'

'What about ... you know ... down there?' she says, treacherously.

Of course, we all look ... you know ... down there.

'What?' he says, suddenly crimson.

She turns to me, conspiratorially. 'He gets up three times in the night. Four times sometimes.'

'It's normal. It's just age,' he pleads.

'I think he should get it checked out,' says his wife, looking at him then back to me. 'Don't you?'

'Probably ... but it's really none of my business.'

'But you're the one with the clipboard,' she points out.

I make my excuses and leave them to continue the heated conversation they've clearly had a hundred times before.

They think the knuckly bit on the thumb might be broken. They also think it's infected and suggest that I go straight to A & E. I go straight to A & E, but the queue to register to join another queue to see a nurse to join another queue to see a doctor is snaking around the block and at least half of it is vomiting into cardboard sick bowls so I decide I'm fine, the antibiotics will kick in any minute, and, if not, I'll try again tomorrow.

'The NHS was built around the people who turned up,' says Ben Sinclair, the doctor we met in the last chapter.

'We capture women when they first come in to discuss contraception. After that, they typically see their GP every six months or so. They're called in for follow-ups and then it's, "By the way, can we just check your blood pressure while you're here?" and "Should we screen for this and check for that?" They're in the system.

'On the other hand, most eighteen-year-old men have never booked their own GP appointment. They don't know how to engage with the system and they aren't asked to engage with it until they're forty. And that's too late. It's too late for heart disease, for diabetes and for STDs.'

Sinclair spent several years at the NHS coalface before setting up his own private clinic. During his time as a GP, his attempts to help patients were limited by the tyranny of the ten-minute appointment. In general, his female patients were quite adept at coming straight to the point, whereas the few men who turned up tended to adopt a more circuitous approach.

'We would start with some minor issue, like an ingrowing toenail,' he says. 'We'd spend most of the allotted time discussing that, I'd offer some advice or write a prescription, and they would stand up to leave. On their way out, they would pause at the door, look back and say, "Actually, I'm really worried about my testicles," or "I think I'm impotent," or, very occasionally, "I can't cope at work."'

Expecting a GP to cure stress, impotence and/or worrying testicles in the last thirty seconds of a regulation ten-minute appointment is, of course, unrealistic, but Sinclair empathises. 'Men have an access barrier,' he says. 'Either they feel like they don't deserve your help or they don't trust you.

They find it hard to talk about personal issues, particularly if those issues are to do with sexual or mental health. They need to build up trust, but they have no relationship with you. They've never seen you before and, in the current NHS system, they will probably never see you again.'

In his private practice, the initial consultation takes an hour – 'the minimum I need to get an overview and devise a life plan'. Sinclair has developed what he calls the Integrated Health Pyramid: your body is linked to your mind, which is linked to your relationships, which are linked to your overall wellbeing, which is linked back to your mind. 'In short,' he explains over an unhealthy pint, 'everything is linked. Say, for example, you play football each week with your mates and then you break your leg. A physical problem becomes a social problem. You have lost the company of those mates. Say that leg doesn't heal quickly. The prolonged social exclusion starts to affect your mental health. If it goes on, you might even find yourself asking more philosophical questions. "Why me? Why now?"'

Sinclair's aim in those luxurious, one-hour appointments is to deal with problems before they arise. Rather than waiting for the chest pains to arrive and then hoping they'll depart, he advocates pre-emptive treatment. 'Because everything is linked, it's essential to look after your physical health and address issues as soon as – or, ideally, before – they occur,' he says.

At this point, I'm braced for the inevitable healthier-lifestyle lecture. Even though we're in a pub, not a surgery, I fully expect Sinclair to launch into a monologue on the dangers of alcohol and the benefits of exercise and vegetables.

I am wrong. Vegetables do not feature. Instead, Sinclair says, 'We need to be kinder to ourselves. Self-compassion is not something we focus on in our culture. Men are built with a powerful win–lose philosophy. We set goals and then we beat ourselves up if we can't achieve those goals. I have plenty of clients working in law, for example. In a large firm, you have hundreds of people striving for success and only very, very few of them can become senior partners. All the others, to varying degrees, feel like they are failures. When we attach too much to that win–lose outlook, it's not healthy. I try to improve people's self-esteem, empower them to appreciate what they're doing right now, appreciate the small things. Set goals, yes, but make them realistic and adjust them if necessary without feeling like a failure.'

So, we need to set *achievable* goals: lose five kilos in the next year, cycle to work twice a week, go vegetarian on Mondays. Or, in Sinclair's case, run through the forest each morning.

Self-compassion also means giving yourself the time and space to understand what's going on. To – try not to gag – check in with yourself. Sinclair tells me about the senior partner at a law firm who came in with a pesky mole on his face and ended up reassessing his (calamitous) work–life balance. In order to consolidate his position at work, he was commuting five hours a day and seeing his family only through the fog of exhausted weekends. After three consultations of gentle coaxing he resigned and found a local job, trading status for happiness. I don't know what happened to the pesky mole.

Sinclair also recalls the time when he was called to a local office to attend to an executive who had fainted, resulting in a nasty fall. It transpired that the executive had a history of fainting. On this occasion, he was standing at his desk when he started to feel faint. Some time later, he collapsed, whacking himself on the edge of the desk on the way down.

'Why some time later?' asked Sinclair. 'Why didn't you sit down when you first felt faint?'

'Because I had to finish an important email.'

A work–life–health-balance conversation ensued. And, because of Sinclair's Everything's Connected Pyramid, they eventually got all the way back to the executive's childhood. It emerged that his mother had become severely depressed after suffering a stillbirth when he was just two years old. With no warning, and none of the acuity he needed to understand what was going on, he was sent to live with relatives for several months. 'He had never thought about the impact of that separation at such an acute point of his development,' says Sinclair. 'After we talked, he began to address the wound it had left, and his fainting fits became less frequent.'

As Sinclair puts it, there should be ten psychologists for every doctor, because so many health problems are psychological rather than physical in origin. In both of these cases, Sinclair gave his patients the time and space they needed to get to the root of a problem they didn't know they had. In both cases, the men had sought help for one issue and received treatment for another. And, in both cases, the examination of their deeper problems was triggered by chance (and facilitated by the time and space afforded by private healthcare).

We need to reach the point where that trigger is unnecessary. We need to seek help even if we don't have a pesky mole or a troublesome toenail to break the ice. We need to discuss our stress, our testicles, our stressed testicles, right at the start of those 10-minute appointments.* Of course, all of this runs counter to the traditional male orthodoxy. It requires us to be kind to ourselves and to accept that we are fallible and might need help.

At the start of this book, several men admitted that they didn't like to think about their happiness (or the lack of it). 'I can't,' you'll recall one of them saying. 'If I start worrying about the meaning of life, I'll go mad.' Many of them took the view that it was better just to keep going, to block out difficult thoughts and ignore ailments. And by 'better', they meant safer – safer to plough on, rather than risk everything unravelling. When I asked for metaphors to describe their lives, they responded with 'plate-spinning', 'a house of cards' and 'dominoes'. There was no time to indulge in the fripperies of feeling.

Very often, I feel the same way. My first brush with therapy – that creepy-voiced relaxation tape and the handful of sessions with my holistic GP – made my teenage insomnia worse before it (or time) made it better. In my twenties and thirties, I adopted an if-it-ain't-broke-don't-analyse-it

---

* This reminds me, obliquely, of a news report I heard on a local radio station when I was living in Australia. There had been a murder or a shark attack or a gas explosion or something, I can't remember – that's not the important bit – and the investigating officer was updating the media. When asked how the person had died, he said, 'There were no obvious signs of injury ... apart from the fact that the victim's head was missing.'

approach, which seemed to work perfectly well. Any friends who sought professional help always seemed to have an easily identifiable problem – postnatal depression, child abandonment issues, the loss of a parent, divorce – whereas there were no obvious skeletons in my Freudian cupboard. Or, if there were, I'd long since whipped them out of there and buried them. Everything was fine. Tra-la-la.

My hand looks like a baboon's bottom. At six o'clock this morning, I'm back in A & E. This time there's no queue, so I see the nurse immediately. She says I'll have to wait till eight to see the doctor. I tell her I feel fine. She tells me I must see the doctor. Three hours later, the doctor says I've probably broken my thumb and I must see an orthopaedic surgeon. An hour after that, the orthopaedic surgeon tells me I have definitely broken my thumb and transacted a ligament. It's an open fracture and there's a risk the forest debris has already got into the bone, which would be bad. I tell him I'm writing a chapter about men's complacency about their health. His colleague tells me her dad handled midlife very badly. We all nod knowingly.

Then came my forties. The early-years parenting crisis was over. I had a minute to think. I realised I was feeling a bit off. Not down, specifically, but certainly tired. If life is like a cross-Channel swim – which it isn't, but let's pretend it is because I've already bored you with the mountain metaphor – then this is the bit in the middle. If you squint forward, you can see Calais (death) on the horizon and, if you squint back, you can see Dover (childhood). You're only halfway across but you're already knackered, not least because you've just swum through a swarm of jellyfish (which, in this increasingly tortured metaphor, is having kids). You're treading water, trying to find the energy to plough on. But for what? Calais? An eternity of nothingness? Neither seems particularly worth it, but what are your options? You can't turn back. You can't tread water indefinitely. What you really need is a nice little mid-Channel island, some unseasonably tropical weather and a sunbed.

A few weeks after my forty-first birthday – an age so thoroughly bleak, so neither here nor there, so depressingly mid-Channel that I refused to mark it in any way – I booked a one-to-one session with a highly recommended 'intuitive therapist'. She would, the high recommenders explained, help me be happy, passionate and in love with life again. She'd be my mid-Channel tropical island. It was worth a shot.

For the whole week before the session, I wanted to cancel; and for the first five minutes of it, I wished I had. In a small room on the top floor of a London townhouse, the therapist began by asking what was wrong and I said that there was nothing in particular and that I wasn't even sure why I was there. I was forty-one, everything felt as set as a three-day-old blancmange and there were, barring a scratch-card win, no more surprises. I started describing the Channel swimmer metaphor but lost my train of thought. 'Oh, and I can't concentrate. I've spent ten years multi-tasking, like every working parent does. I can do many things, but I can't do one thing. I have forgotten what it's like to read a book in two sittings or watch a film in one.' To all of which she smiled and said, 'Allow your thoughts to be here, but when your mind tries to take control, just say, "I surrender."'

Which made me want to leave even more.

After an unspecified period – possibly days – of awkward silence, she then told me to connect with my heart. 'You might not have done this for a while,' she said. 'It's safer and easier with the brain.'

As I struggled with this just like I struggled when my wife told me to listen to my heart – what does she mean, what is the point? – the smiling therapist moved her chair so we were facing each other. 'Hold my gaze,' she said. 'Do not look away.' Try this at home, preferably with a loved one rather than a total stranger. Set up facing chairs, take a seat and stare at each other for five minutes. No laughing or joking. Serious face. It's incredibly hard. After a minute, you'll start fighting the urge to look away. 'Honour your resistance,' she told me. After two minutes, absurd thoughts like 'This is unbearably intimate' and 'We're going to have to get married now' will float in and out of your head. 'Connect with your heart, not your head,' she repeated. After five minutes, your brain or your heart, no idea, will have accepted the situation in which it finds itself.

For me, that acceptance was followed rapidly and inexplicably by a sense of feeling overwhelmed. She told me I was blocked creatively and asked if I could feel the blocks. I tried to answer but my voice cracked, so I stopped. I blinked furiously at welling tears and asked for a minute's pause. I was embarrassed. I only ever cry when Nick

Knowles shows the refurbished house to the struggling family at the end of *DIY SOS*.

I didn't go back for a second session. I should have – the therapist said there was work to do and she was probably right – but I left feeling strangely elated, wandered around in a daze for a few hours and, by the following morning, had convinced myself that I'd had a cathartic experience, touched some deep emotion, given my midlife malaise a good kick in the teeth and now, really, everything was fine. In all honesty, though, I was afraid. Not of dredging up one of those non-existent skeletons but of signing up for a prolonged wallow in undeserved self-pity. I'd been brought to tears because a complete stranger was, in a very intensive way, offering to help. I didn't need help.

If men are reluctant to address their physical health, a whole new layer of stigma encases their mental health. Even the suggestion of seeking 'professional help' sets many of my fragile interviewees on edge.

According to the most recent NHS statistics, one in five women suffers from anxiety or depression, compared with one in eight men. Yet, men are three times more likely to take their own lives. Attempts have been made to explain this apparent incongruity by linking men's relatively high suicide rate to their tendency to resort to violence in general. This may be true but surely the fact that men are less likely to admit to – and seek help for – mental illness is also a factor. How else to explain that men are also three times more likely to become alcohol or drug dependent?

'Male anxiety and depression present in a completely different way to women, and it's a scandal how this means they are all but ignored,' Martin Pollecoff, chair of the UK Council for Psychotherapy, told *The Times* in 2019. 'If you look at the *Diagnostic and Statistical Manual of Mental Disorders*, which is the bible for diagnosing mental-health conditions, there are eight hundred pages of symptoms women will readily recognise because they express feelings, but few for men, whose behaviours under stress can be quite displaced. It's a terrible thing to say, but women feel and men act out. They slope off to the pub, smoke a joint, start a fight, see a prostitute. Anxious men tend to lose themselves. And then the awful thing is, their anxiety is not diagnosed and we end up in this terrible situation where the first time we know something is wrong is when they take their own lives.'

Four decades ago, Gary Barker, then a seventeen-year-old Texan schoolboy, witnessed a classmate shoot and kill another classmate in the high school cafeteria. 'I knew the two young men,' he tells me in his office in Washington, DC. 'They had bullying issues and they had grade issues ... They were two guys you would cross the hallway to avoid. You could tell there were storms brewing in their heads and that what they needed was help. But their problems were addressed with discipline and control.'

Although Barker would go on to dedicate his life to understanding and countering the effects of toxic masculinity, it took years for him to address, let alone process, what had happened. In the immediate aftermath, none of the young men or women in the cafeteria received grief counselling. 'The boys were allowed to hug their girlfriends,' Barker says. 'The girls cried and the boys just looked at the ground before being sent back to class. Even today, we still pathologise this sort of thing. These perpetrators are damaged human beings but we use words like "monster" and "evil". We bring out the Bible in order to separate them from us and to avoid understanding what happened and what we are going to do about it.'

The shooting remained 'unaddressed background noise' for Barker until, as a twentysomething developmental psychologist, he began working in conflict areas in Colombia, Brazil and the Congo: 'I was spending every day with other survivors of trauma and, for the first time, I started talking about it.' After coordinating studies on child survivors of violence and the sexual exploitation of girls, he began to ask what was – and to a certain degree still is – a controversial question: when do we involve men in the conversation? 'How could you have a meaningful discussion about domestic violence, sexual exploitation and school shootings without also having a discussion about manhood?' he wonders.

Since then, Promundo, the organisation Barker established in the poorest areas of Rio de Janeiro, has developed programmes in more than forty countries. Many ministries of health and education have incorporated its activities into their programmes. Barker himself has advised the UN, the World Bank and numerous governments and international foundations on 'strategies to engage men and boys in promoting gender equality'. All of this came from that very simple, very unfashionable axiom: if we're going to make the world a better place, we need to involve men in the process.

'There has been opposition,' Barker admits. 'There is a worry that in some parts of the world, even in our supposedly advanced Western democracies, the full equality promised to women has not been achieved. Many of the women's rights organisations that we partner with think that if men begin to get into this space, we're going to recentre this work to make it about us. That is, after all, what men are really good at. If we say we're the victims of the patriarchy too, it will become all about us.'

I suggest the women's rights organisations may have a point.

They do, says Barker. but if we don't get away from this binary view of power, then 'we're just remaking the battle of the sexes. It's boring: we get stuck and it reinforces the very things we're trying to break. Men are suffering tremendously. That doesn't mean that women aren't making twenty per cent less than men and that we're eighty per cent of those who are in power and that we're still suffering.'

In a landmark study of young men in Mexico, the United Kingdom and the United States, sponsored (unironically) by Axe,* Barker and his team identified a set of beliefs that contributes to a traditional and frequently damaging version of masculinity. 'Communicated by parents, families, the media, peers, and other members of society, these beliefs

---

* Axe – or Lynx to you and me – still has a way to go to rebrand itself as anything close to enlightened. In 2016, the manufacturer, Unilever, promised to ditch the deodorant's infamous sexist image after research showed that only 2 per cent of its adverts featured intelligent women. Since then, teenage boys have had to manage without the comforting fantasy that one spray of the pungent fragrance will trigger a stampede of beautiful women.

place pressure on men to be a certain way,' the researchers concluded. 'These pressures tell men to be self-sufficient, to act tough, to be physically attractive, to stick to rigid roles, to be heterosexual, to have sexual prowess, and to use aggression to resolve conflicts.' The respondents who held these beliefs were trapped in what the researchers called 'the Man Box'. The study showed that this Man Box, this set of socially reinforced rules about what 'real men' should do, is still alive and well in the developed world.

'In all three countries, eighteen- to thirty-year-old men are on board, more or less, with the idea that women are their equals,' Barker explains. 'There is also a pretty good acceptance of sexual diversity. But there's still a lot of currency with this tough-guy, don't-show-your-vulnerabilities version of manhood.' In other words, the latest generation of young men is edging out of the box when it comes to its view of other people, but still very much in it when it comes to its view of itself.

Barker notes that the Man Box survey was carried out just before the Brexit referendum and just before Donald Trump was elected. 'This tough-guy version of manhood is what Trump ran on, and some of the Brexiteers have run on a similar platform – the idea that *we* are working-class men and *they* are taking our jobs,' he says. So, to some extent, we could attribute those political earthquakes of 2016 to 'some kind of [perceived] challenge to masculinity'.

Confusingly, the men who are still firmly inside the Man Box display both more depressive tendencies and more happiness. That happiness, Barker says, is fleeting: 'If we live with those tropes of a manly man, then we feel a sense of happiness when we achieve them. Look at how full our gyms are – more so than they were twenty years ago. We have to look a certain way, dress a certain way, have the correct amount of body hair. If we do, we are successful on Tinder.' The depressive tendencies are more intractable. The belief that you must never show weakness is deeply ingrained, even in men who have escaped other aspects of traditional masculinity.

Promundo runs 'Manhood 2.0' workshops, and Barker says they work: 'If a group of fifteen- to eighteen-year-olds hang out with us through a cycle of eight classes, we consistently see change.' According to Barker, each workshop has its own *Matrix* moment. Just as Neo clocks that he's a human blood battery wired into a malevolent machine, the young men suddenly understand that the traditional version of manhood is a farce: 'One guy will open up about how he feels, the others will pitch in and say, "Wow, that's exactly how I feel too," and they realise collectively that they have all built up armour and they all wish they could escape it.'

At which point, I think, Perfect, this is how we'll do it. It might be too late for my generation – we're stuck with the chest-clutching, telling-wife-we're-fine form of unhealthy, manly manhood. But if we can get to the next lot and prove that the John Wayne routine doesn't work in the long run, all will be well.

Sadly, Barker is quick to burst that particular bubble. 'It works until you get back into the real world and your mates don't want to hear about your feelings,' he says.

'So we need to start even earlier?'

'Yes.'

'How early?'

'At its simplest level, we put capes on toddlers and tell them they are superheroes,' he says. 'We show them that the world expects a performance from them: be tough, win by defeating others, show no weakness. "Aren't you my little man?" In those early years, your mother is the safe place where you can run when you fall over and don't want your friends to see you crying in your superhero costume. Eventually, we transfer that to a long-term partner, but not always and only after years of battened-down hatches.'

Promundo is trialling workshops with these young super-heroes. Eight- to ten-year-old boys, says Barker, are still carrying their mothers' message – that it's okay to be vul-nerable – but by eleven or twelve, 'the male peer group has taken over: "If I show anything less than the stereotypical version of manhood, my mates will make fun of me." You watch them paint the suit of armour on thick.'

Most of the middle-aged men I've interviewed for this book have made great strides from their fathers' generation. The stiff upper lip is no longer the first rule of being a man. But that's left us in a confusing, mixed-message stage of masculinity. Emotionally, we're still old school, and this has huge ramifications for the way we deal with the stresses and strains of midlife.

It's easy to say we should be more honest with our loved ones and ourselves, that we should accept our own fragility, that we should ask for help, but even if we take those steps, are those around us ready for it? Will our partners listen? Will our friends? Will healthcare professionals?

Over the last decade, the trickle of household names admitting to mental health issues has become a flood, and campaigns such as Movember – 'changing the face of men's health' – have helped to destigmatise fallibility. But there is a long way to go. Men still tend to mask their depression, or it manifests as irritability, anger, miserable silence, heavy drinking or, in the worst cases, violence, rather than the extreme, debilitating sadness that depressed women tend to report to their GPs. 'There doesn't seem to be any biological basis to explain why mental health issues would manifest themselves in different ways for men and women,' says Barker. 'We think those differences are about the socially acceptable ways that men and women manifest mental health needs.'

It is also too simplistic, he adds, to say that men are more likely to take their own lives because of their greater propensity for violence. 'Typically, in the research on survivors, you see an economic stress issue or a previous mental health issue in men, but you also get "I didn't think I could ask for help" or "I didn't want to ask for help." While women see a call for help as a call for help, men see it as further evidence of failed masculinity. It's an additional inducement of shame. The only way out is to be successful in a suicide attempt.'

My thumb is fine, thanks for asking. The infection is over. But I need to book a virtual appointment at the virtual fracture clinic to discuss a possible operation to reconnect the ligament. 'What will happen if I just leave it?' I ask a friend who works in operating theatres.

'Don't leave it,' he says, using his own crooked finger as a handy example. 'Get it sorted out. You've got almost half a life ahead of you.'

I'm still inclined to leave it. Not because I'm unwilling to accept my own fragility. It's just that having an operation is, literally and logistically, a huge pain. Drs Sinclair and Barker both talk about the obstacles to treatment for men. But when it comes down to it, I reckon it's as much about finding the time as anything else.

Time. That word always crops up whenever I think about these things. Or rather the lack of it. I could sort out the garden. I could fix my thumb. I could play more football with the kids. I could be healthier. I could be happier. If only I had more time.

At the extreme ends of physical and mental health, it is easy enough to urge men to take action. Of course, the man with the chest pains should see a doctor. Of course, the man suffering bouts of irrational anger should see a psychotherapist. But in the mundane middle, where everything is basically okay but not great, where it is possible just to keep going, then keeping going always wins. Not least because keeping going is safer. It means we don't have to address the one deep issue that frames everyone's midlife.

Until now, most of us have felt invincible, immortal even. Now, though, it is harder to live with that pretence. Our own mortality has become harder to ignore – hair is receding, testosterone is dropping, backs are creaking, energy is draining, physical decline is becoming undeniable. If we were sensible, we would accept this and adapt to it. Instead, we tell ourselves we don't have the time. This is just an excuse for inaction, for focusing on the urgent rather than the important, for neglect, for denial. The reality is that there is *always* time. We just have to be prepared to find it and accept the consequences.

CHAPTER SEVEN

Men and technology

It's 2062 and the apocalypse finally arrived a couple of years ago. It wasn't the full Hollywood zombie apocalypse. No vastly superior aliens landed. In the less spectacular end, this was a more Roman decline and fall of civilisation as we knew it. Things just got out of hand. Too many magic money trees. Too much consumption. One extended loan, one upgrade, one glitch too far and ... *Bang* – the total and irretrievable collapse of our vastly overcomplicated techno-capitalist system.*

Here in 2062, there are no cars, no planes, no internet,

---

* I'm writing this at what is, hopefully, several weeks after the peak of the coronavirus pandemic. Garden centres have reopened and everything. By the time this book is published, I assume that most of us will have resumed our normal, busy, high-consuming lifestyles ... although I hope that's not the case. Either way, the crisis has demonstrated just how fragile global society really is.

no ready meals and no electric kettles. Humans are still trying to come to terms with a world where Mars bars, Nespresso capsules and *DIY SOS* no longer exist. It isn't all bad, though. There are no traffic wardens either.

My post-apocalyptic home is a geodesic dome by a lake somewhere south of what used to be the buzzing cosmopolitan metropolis of Birmingham. In the absence of Homebase, the dome was constructed entirely from materials foraged from the recent hi-tech past. Rusting car panels have been cut into triangles and riveted together to form the outer shell. The inner skin is recycled chipboard. It's the kind of place Mad Max would book for a staycation.

Inside, make-do-and-mend has replaced Amazon Prime. There's an ancient wood burner for warmth and cooking, and a disappointingly weak solar-powered lamp to illuminate the slow evenings. I also have a stockpile of tinned food and an exceedingly out-of-date mountain of Mr Kipling's French Fancies. I have no iPlayer, radiators or whisky, but I do have books (well thumbed), firewood (diminishing) and home-brew beer (quite drinkable after the first three difficult pints).

This dome is real, even if the apocalypse isn't ... yet. It's called The Clearing and it stands on the edge of a beautiful lake in the grounds of Compton Verney, a stately home in Warwickshire. Two artists, Tom James and Alex Hartley, conceived and designed it three years ago to show visitors what we might lose – and gain – in the increasingly likely event that everything goes awry for humanity.

As one of the project's volunteer caretakers, I was there for a week to keep the place running and explain to visitors what on earth was going on. By day three, I was starting to tire of the tinned beans and the not-very-Viennese whirls, but I had warmed to my role as a sort of apocalyptic National Trust warden. It was fascinating to see people's reactions to this particular take on our potential future. Without exception, the more senior citizens became immediately nostalgic. They regaled me with tales of the blissfully tech-free past, of ye olde butchers, bakers and candlestick makers. Ahh, those glorious days when there were only two television channels, two motorway lanes and two pints of milk on the doorstep each morning.

'Technology hasn't made life easier,' said one chap in an unashamedly striped blazer and Panama hat, almost certainly not for the first time. 'You can keep your internet banking, your Kindles and your call centres. I'd be happy sitting by this lake with a good book.'

Curiously, all of the younger visitors – the digital natives – agreed with the oldies. They loved the idea of living in the dome, pottering about in the vegetable patch and playing pass the turnip of a long autumn evening. Each time one of them gave their little teacher's-pet monologue about how life would be better if there were less technology, I'd hit them with the killer question: 'But you wouldn't have that phone. Or an iPad. Or a Nintendo Switch. Or TikTok. Are you sure you could manage?'

'Yes,' they would reply, without hesitation.

It is possible that they might change their minds after a few analogue days, but their joy at the idea of playing tech-free survival in a recycled dome was convincingly unbridled. One thoughtful boy even pointed out that it was 'like Minecraft live'.

It fell to the midlifers, my miserable age group, to burst the enthusiastic bubble. Half of them took ostrich-like exception to the whole idea of an imminent techno-apocalypse: 'It will never happen ... we can invent our way out of any catastrophe.' Hmm. The other half adopted an air of resignation before they'd even settled on the repurposed car seats: 'We learnt nothing from the last financial crisis ... I doubt an art installation is going to change anyone's mind ... All our government can do is ban single-use plastic bags – bloody useless.' Denial and resignation: the two cornerstones of the midlife struggle.

I might have been exactly the same if I'd been visiting rather than staying. But, as the week progressed, at the speed of the proverbial asthmatic ant carrying heavy shopping, I had time to form a less impulsive, less panicked response.

One huge advantage of the impending collapse of modern society appears to be that we will have more leisure time. There will still be chores to do, of course, and without the aid of dishwashers, washing machines, vacuum cleaners and hair straighteners. Plus, it turns out, composting toilets don't look after themselves. Food must be grown. Water-filtration systems must be maintained. Broken things must be mended. But no one will be pulling a fifty-hour week.

Instead, claim the artists behind the project, we would return to something approximating the pre-industrial work–life balance. Back then, as the sociologist Juliet Schor has argued, 'the tempo of life was slow, even leisurely; the pace of work relaxed. Our ancestors may not have been rich, but they had an abundance of leisure.'

The medieval working day stretched from dawn to dusk, regardless of the season: eight hours in the winter, sixteen in the summer. Ouch. But the toil was intermittent. Your average peasant would have a long breakfast, a long lunch, a long afternoon nap and a long dinner, with extra breaks in the morning and afternoon for good measure. Annual leave was generous, too: Christmas, Easter, midsummer, copious saints' days and 'ale weeks' to mark weddings, christenings, deaths and harvests added up to at least a third of a year bunking off.

Bring on the apocalypse, I wrote in my notebook towards the end of my stay. That obviously didn't age well so let's temper it for pandemic times. Bring on a more leisurely cycle of life. Banish time scarcity. Declutter. Unboot. Unplug. Downgrade. Yes, there are still a couple of low-tech spanners in the works. If the world's multinational manufacturing systems collapsed, so too would our multi-national pharmaceutical companies. Medicine and medical treatment would not revert entirely to the pustular days of the Dark Ages, but you wouldn't be able to pop a couple of Nurofen the morning after too much of that home-brew. Dentistry would be tricky, too – some clove oil and a hand drill? Hip replacements, pacemakers, statins, keyhole surgery, chemotherapy and vaccines would all go because they are too high tech. We would die younger. But who wouldn't trade a few miserable years at the end if all the years up to then were happier?

Willing an apocalypse is not the most practical way to

improve life. Wishing we could have the work–life balance of a peasant is more of a long-term aspiration than a quick-fix remedy for midlife misery. But the two things that made my time in the geodesic dome so enjoyable are the two things all of us can embrace now without any great upheaval. First, less tech. Second, more physical work.

Technology makes life more – not less – stressful. This is what every middle-aged person has said since the dawn of middle-aged men. If we could take a time machine back to the invention of the wheel, we'd find two old curmudgeons sitting in a cave round the corner moaning about how life was much, much better when carts just scraped along the ground. But the pace at which technology has come to dominate our lives over the last few decades is mind-blowing. My generation has had to cope with the leap from vinyl to CD, from typewriter to word processor, and from analogue TV to digital TV. Now we have to get our heads around the idea of sentient fridges, too.

Things really started to go wrong when phones got smart. That was the moment when our legislators should have said, 'No, sorry, Steve. This is the wrong direction for humanity. We should not be walking around with supercomputers in our pockets. No good will come of it.'

They missed that opportunity. Smartphones got smart and then the smartness spread. It found its way into our living rooms, our kitchens and our bedrooms. It was not enough that our phones and computers were communicating with each other. Everything else had to join the conversation too – light switches, speakers, smoke alarms, doorbells, key rings, fitness trackers, baby monitors, watches, vacuum cleaners, toys, vibrators – all under the cover of making our lives easier.

Being a curmudgeonly midlifer myself, I have always been ill-disposed towards the Internet of Things. I held out for years as everyone around me started talking to inanimate objects until, a year ago, in a moment of madness, I bought a smart thermostat. 'It will be great,' I convinced myself. 'I'll be able to turn the heating on before I get home. I won't have to fumble around in the airing cupboard every time I want to tweak the settings. I can do it all on an app on my phone.' Here's a simple rule that will guarantee a better life: if you're thinking of buying something that needs an app, don't buy it. On that fateful evening, I forgot that rule.

For the first three months, the new thermostat was, as billed, smart. The daily 'Did you remember to turn the heating off?' argument was no more because I could simply get out my phone and check. Then, in early November, very much like it had watched *The Lawnmower Man*, like it thought it knew better, the smart thermostat put itself into 'learning mode'. Quietly, surreptitiously, it began to develop a mind of its own. If it disagreed with my heating strategy for the week, it would revise it. It had a medieval monk's approach to energy use in the morning but went full Polish grandmother in the evening. It took to putting the heating on every time it sensed someone was in the house, which would have been clever, except that 'someone' included cats, spiders, slight draughts, spectral entities, firework displays and burglars. If we are going to get burgled, I'd rather the burglar didn't get to do his burgling at the optimum room temperature.

After several increasingly desperate factory-setting res-
torations and a whole afternoon of customer-service 'live
chat' (ironically, it's impossible to talk to another real-life
human in the Information Age), I finally managed to disa-
ble the learning mode. It didn't like that at all. For the next
few weeks, it would switch on the heating in the middle
of the night and turn it off an hour before dawn. For the
rest of the winter, it sulked. It was the petulant teenager of
thermostats.

Not long after smashing it to pieces, I'm interviewing
Baroness Kidron, the BAFTA-winning filmmaker and children's rights campaigner, about a new piece of legislation
she and her colleagues are introducing in an effort to keep
kids safe online. I mention my recent struggles with the
smart thermostat and Kidron takes a deep breath, like a
teacher who is about to explain long division to a baboon:
'If you click through everyone with whom that thermostat
company shares your data, it's a thousand sets of terms and
conditions you've automatically agreed to,' she says, citing
research by the University of London. 'If it does not worry
you that your household details are being shared with at
least a thousand companies, then fine. But if you put a thousand people in your house and asked them to stand silently
watching what you and your family were doing, you might
feel differently.'

That's not the problem. Well, it is. The fact that multi-
national companies are harvesting our data and using it to
influence us for the good of their profit margins rather than
our wellbeing is not ideal. But the bigger problem is that it's
all such an enormous, monstrous, exasperating faff. We've

already established that time – or the lack of it – is a press-ing issue. And smart devices are marketed as time-savers. In reality, they do the opposite. They intrude, they pollute, they corrupt. They waste our time.

Even if you manage to find a smart thermostat that isn't bent on ruining your life, one cold bath at a time, it will still make its presence felt. It will send notifications. Do you want to update? Do you want two-step verification to protect your data, data you didn't want to create in the first place because it's ... just ... a ... thermostat?* Do you want to compare your energy usage to that of other smart thermostat users in your area? It might even style itself as the Greta Thunberg of central heating, rewarding you with meaningless 'bonus points' if you use less electricity than your profligate neighbours.

Then there's a new challenge: the Cloud. I have lost whole afternoons to an ongoing battle with this omnipo-tent, mystical, cirrocumulus force. Once your music, your photos and your digital detritus are stored in the ether, it's very hard to get them back down again. I have come to believe that it's just easier to avoid the Cloud altogether, but none of my devices agree. The minute I'm not looking, one of them starts sneaking things into orbit. If I'm not

---

* If I could just get back the time I've wasted trying to remember passwords and answers to allegedly memorable questions, I would be time rich. Is it the old password or the new one? Or the other one I used after reading an article about Russian hackers upsetting toddlers through smart baby monitors? Does it have an exclamation mark? Is it upper case? What colour was my first car? What is the name of my wife's first pet? Number of words from Marx as revolutionary duo iffy – habitual adulation and dubious mythologies died away? (2,1,4,3,3,1,9,4,5,3,4,2,7,2).

quick to stop it, the others quickly follow suit. Thousands of photos and music files float away. Files that have been deleted on a new iPhone but still exist on an old iPhone are beamed up to the Cloud and back down to all the bloody iPhones. The first I know about this is an email: 'You are using 49GB of your Cloud. If you want to use more than 50GB, please send us more cash.' It is the digital version of sorting out all the junk in the garage, driving it to the dump, then returning home to find it all back in the garage while the random bloke who put it there asks you for a tenner.

In 2005, before household objects got smart and when iPhones and iPads were just twinkles in Steve Jobs's eye, three computer scientists at the University of California, Irvine measured the effect of minor interruptions, such as the arrival of an email in your inbox. They found that it took almost twenty minutes, on average, to regain momentum. Fifteen years of rampant technological 'advancement' later, the mere idea of twenty uninterrupted minutes seems laughable. Between the emails, the texts, the WhatsApp messages, the Slacks and, very occasionally, the good old-fashioned phone calls, most of us spend every waking minute in a state of permanent distraction. A smart watch interrupts a smartphone interrupts a smart speaker interrupts a smart fitness tracker interrupts a conversation you were trying to have with your children about the dangers of technology.

News flash: it's easier to stick with the dumb thermostat in the cupboard. It's easier to switch your lights on with a switch and to tell the time with a watch and to answer the door with yourself, not a wireless virtual avatar of yourself.*

I had no distractions once the day-trippers had left the geodesic dome. I was left with pure analogue time to myself. I didn't know what to do with it for the first couple of days, but then, not out of choice, I started to relax. I sat on the deck. I watched the sun set. I watched the stars and (harrumph) satellites slide across the sky. I went for a morning stroll, an afternoon stroll and an evening stroll. I went for another stroll. I felt bored. I felt good about feeling bored. I sat on the deck again. And that pure analogue time stretched out ahead of me. It was no longer a luxury, no longer intruded upon by needy technology. Delicate circadian rhythms, trammelled by a life of blue light, returned at first hesitantly, then more forcefully. Time slowed down and seemed abundant. On the fourth night, I slept for nine hours straight and still woke at dawn. I haven't done that since I was six years old.

---

* 'Wireless', while we're talking about time-saving, is another lie. You still need a cable to charge your supposedly wireless gadget and another to connect it to other devices when its wirelessness fails. I'm prepared to put money on you having a drawer, maybe two drawers, maybe a whole loft, full of cables, all knotted together like hellish techno-spaghetti. Mains, USB, micro-USB, mini-USB, USB 2.0, USB 3.0, USB 2.0–USB 3.0, HDMI, DVI-I, DVI-D, kettle, toaster, display port and so on. Some of these are obsolete, others are not, but no normal person has any way of knowing which is which. When Apple decided that the 3.5mm headphone jack should go in the dustbin of history, it consigned a billion or so pairs of headphones to the spaghetti loft. And when the European Commission asked tech companies to agree on one standard charging cable, its sensible, environmentally attuned, user-friendly plan met with intransigence. That was back in 2009 and the tech companies are still refusing to comply.

As a result, my time in the apocalypse was not unlike a proper getting-away-from-it-all holiday. It was the sort of escape twenty-first-century workers crave. 'Digital detox' is now a marketable concept. It is why you find 'no Wi-Fi' listed as an amenity on the more bijou camping websites and why there was so much resistance when airlines first started offering Wi-Fi on planes. The 'it' in 'getting away from it all' used to mean work, stress, credit-card statements, the bureaucratic grind of life. Now it means all of that plus technology. An analogue break is a luxury. Which begs the question: why have it in the first place? Why do we welcome all these digital devices into our lives and then plan ways to escape them?

Now, I know there's no shortage of 'digital detox plans' on YouTube. (On. You. Tube.) The foot soldiers of the 'you can have it all' brigade are especially keen on the idea. No phones after 7 p.m. No tech of any sort at any time in the bedroom. Check your emails once a day, or twice if you must. Delete all of your social media accounts. Cancel Netflix. All of this is perfectly reasonable advice. But, for middle-aged men in particular, it fails to address the dominant emotion behind our need to stay connected. Fear.

The subject of smartphones comes up in almost every conversation about work–life balance. Checking them is the first thing these stressed, exhausted, professional people do in the morning and the last thing they do at night. They are well aware that this pollutes their pure time at home, but when I suggest 'no phones after 7 p.m.' or at least the setting of strict parameters, there is resistance. They need to keep an eye on things. They're only checking there's nothing urgent. If they don't check, they worry, which defeats the object of not checking in the first place. And besides, they have a boss or a client who expects a near-instantaneous response, no matter what time of day or night it is.

If I push this further and ask if they've ever tried being a little less instantaneous, the answer is always no. It's not worth the risk. End of discussion. In an ideal world, our employers would understand that we want and need to have boundaries. In an even more ideal world, we would be willing to test that.

A decade ago, when Hanna Rosin was researching her landmark essay 'The End of Men', she sat in on a court-mandated class for fathers who had failed to pay child support in Kansas City.

'The men in that room, almost without exception, were casualties of the end of the manufacturing era,' she observed. 'Most of them had continued to work with their hands even as demand for manual labor was declining. Since 2000 [i.e. in the first decade of the twenty-first century] manufacturing [in the United States] has lost almost six million jobs, more than a third of its total workforce, and has taken in few young workers. The housing bubble masked this new reality for a while, creating work in construction and related industries. Many of the men I spoke with had worked as electricians or builders; one had been a successful real-estate agent. Now those jobs are gone too.'

In the UK, the shift away from manufacturing (and, with it, manual labour) has been equally dramatic. In 1968, two-thirds of households were classified as blue collar and/or low paid. By 2000, this had shrunk to less than half. Newspapers ran celebratory stories hailing the rise of a new Britain – a nation of latte-drinking, middle-class office workers.

Of course, there are plenty of benefits to mass white-collar employment. Affluence is one. Workplace health and safety is another. Nobody ever died from a paper cut. But what about the cost? In the evolutionary blink of an eye, the typical working life has become entirely sedentary. We don't make things. We click and tap things. The closest we get to physical labour is making the tea.

Last year, behavioural futurist William Higham and a team of occupational health experts surveyed more than three thousand office workers in France, Germany and the UK. Half of them suffered backache, headaches, eye strain and/or stiff necks. A significant number also had sore legs and various swollen bits and bobs. Helpfully, the team made a manikin to illustrate how the office worker of the future might look. 'Emma' was the stuff of dystopian nightmares. She had a hunched back, sallow skin, swollen wrists and pronounced cankles. Her thin smile didn't extend to her bloodshot eyes. Even by a manikin's standards, she looked bored.

'Unless we make radical changes to our working lives, such as moving more, addressing our posture at our desks, taking regular walking breaks or considering improving our workstation setup, our offices are going to make us very sick,' concluded the rocket scientist (sorry, behavioural futurist).

A key solution, according to Higham's study – which was

sponsored by a company that sells office equipment – was to buy better office equipment. Fine, if a little convenient. But standing desks are not going to make up for almost two decades cooped up in a classroom followed by four or five decades stuck in an office. Going to the gym at lunch might help with the cankles, but what we really need is some way to satisfy our primal urge to do something constructive with our hands.

I realised how much we'd surrendered for a life of convenience during my week in the apocalypse dome. The days were filled with simple, physical tasks. I chopped wood, I made fire, I cooked on the fire, I mended the fence, I hand-swept the dome, I handwashed my plates and, separately, my underpants. With the possible exception of the fence-mending, there's an element of automation in all of these tasks back in the real world. A dishwasher does the dishwashing. A supermarket does the food. A boiler does the heat (if your thermostat permits). All to give us more time to do what, exactly?

A month after my return from the 2060s, we got a quote for some panelling in our entrance hall. It was a ridiculous quote – aimed squarely at people who are pretentious enough to want panelling in their hall. So I decided to do it myself and, over the next six weeks, that's precisely what I did. There were moments of doubt. There were prolonged bouts of profanity. There was, on two occasions, significant blood loss. But if you come to our house, we will welcome you warmly, although you won't notice because you'll be distracted by the lovely panelling.

'Nice panelling,' you will say. 'Is it original?'

And I will look coyly at the floor and say, 'No, I did it.'

And you will look incredulous and say, 'Really?'

And I will say, 'Yes. It was actually quite straightforward.'

Then I will whisk you through to the kitchen before you start to look too closely.

In the Age of Technology, we have deprived ourselves of physical work and the satisfaction of completing it. The impact on our physical health is well documented, but the damage it does to our mental health is also increasingly evident. Conversely, reintroducing physical work – finite jobs with achievable goals rather than twelve-hour shifts down a coal mine – quickly repairs the damage of our sedentary Sisyphean office-based lives.

Or it did for me. And it did for David, 54, a company owner who was on the brink of a proper, old-fashioned midlife crisis when I first interviewed him two years ago. 'I was working sixty-hour weeks trying to keep the business afloat,' he tells me. 'We're a retail company and we were getting killed by e-commerce. My response was to keep slogging away, working longer and longer hours, like I could somehow beat Amazon at its own game if I just stayed in the office longer. It got to the point where I never saw my family and, when I did, I was unable to concentrate on them. I had these spiralling thoughts about what would happen if I lost everything. I didn't realise that the way I was living was effectively the same as losing everything anyway.'

After yet another dark night of the soul, David sold his semi-detached house in north London and bought a cottage in Hertfordshire. It was four hundred years old, and not in a good way. No central heating, no roof, only one inhabitable-ish room.

'Everyone put it down to a midlife crisis,' he says. 'And I suppose it was. But I realised I'd got so caught up with my business that I just wasn't enjoying life any more. I needed something I could focus on that didn't involve spreadsheets, emails and endless unhappy meetings with suppliers.'

All the proceeds of the downsizing were used to restructure the company's debt, which means 'getting a man in' is not an option. David does all the work on the cottage himself. 'I had done DIY before but this was on a different scale,' he says. 'It's a listed building so I have to do everything with traditional materials, under the watchful gaze of a thoroughly disapproving housing officer.'

Two years on, almost half of the cottage is habitable. There is a roof but still no central heating. David is at the point in the *Grand Designs* episode where Kevin McCloud arrives in the rain, scratches his chin and asks penetrating questions about the budget that make the wife cry. But this isn't that kind of story. There is already a happy ending.

'I was forced by the dilapidated state of both the cottage and my own mental health to take a step back at work,' David says. 'I gave up on becoming the next Mike Ashley, which was never a particularly healthy goal anyway, and scaled it all down. I delegated at work, I trusted people around me and I changed focus. Weekends and evenings that used to be spent staring unproductively at the computer screen are now spent poring over nerdy restoration manuals. These days, I have dreams about hydraulic lime mortar rather than nightmares about balance sheets.'

He shows me an old oak-beamed ceiling he hand-chipped free from 1970s plaster and a once-flooded living-room nook that he has restored with such skill and love that a character from *Wolf Hall* would feel right at home. 'You know that adage: no one on their death bed ever wished they'd spent more time in the office?' he asks. 'That's obviously true, but there's work and then there's work. This project is different. I'm proud that this cottage will be here long after I've gone, far prouder than any business success would have made me. I've saved it ... and it's saved me.'

That's how I feel about my panelling. To a lesser degree, sure, but even lesser degrees are important. In fact, they may be more important. We can't all make radical, high-risk changes to our lives, as David did, but we can all make tweaks. A bit of DIY and a forest run here, a gratitude list and the wilful destruction of a smart thermostat there. With enough tweaks, we can tip the happy–miserable see-saw of middle age in our favour.

As I write, my de-teching continues. I'm not in a position to bin my smartphone altogether, but I have stopped checking my emails first thing in the morning and last thing at night. It took rather longer to stop worrying about the fact that I was not checking my emails at those times. I have missed some important missives and failed to nip some nippable crises, but, overall, it has been worth it. Nobody has died or – worse – been fired.

I am almost entirely offline at weekends, and in my post-post-apocalyptic life I have learnt to tile (quite well), to restore stained glass (badly), to carpent (an admittedly basic window seat) and to lay a brick wall (three bricks high). Next summer, I will try my hand at landscape gardening, because no one on their death bed ever wished they'd spent less time in a digger.

CHAPTER EIGHT

Men and money

In 1906, the American philosopher and psychologist William James described 'the moral flabbiness born of the exclusive worship of the bitch-goddess success'* in a chirpy letter to his mate H. G. Wells. 'That – with the squalid cash interpretation put on the word "success" – is our national disease,' he wrote.

One hundred and thirteen years later, I was into the second hour of a visit to a kitchen showroom, listening to the salesman describe the many pros and very few cons of Corian. At that moment, I would have given the salesman

---

* It's unfortunate James decided that 'success' was female. In his day, just as today, worshipping material success to the exclusion of all else was very much a masculine trait. This oversight ruins an otherwise excellent quotation, my use of which has pissed off my wife, so this footnote is for her: I know he's being a dick, but his point is spot on.

all of the money in my bank account to stop talking about Corian. At the end of the second hour, I did.

Even before the longest two hours of my life, this eye-watering purchase was inevitable. Because this was the 'forever' kitchen in the 'forever' house. This was it. I would never spend another penny on a kitchen ever again. Apart from the taps, of course. The following weekend, I spent two hours in the tap showroom. But that was *definitely* it. Our terrifying outgoings would stop laughing in the face of our paltry incomings. I would stop waking up in the night shouting: 'But I did a spreadsheet.' I would stop worshipping the bitch-goddess. I would go on a moral diet and lose a bit of the moral flabbiness around my moral midriff.

Nonsense, of course. The Corian money was just another shovel-load of debt. Another hole on the ever-tightening belt. Another eye roll from the mortgage broker. The etymology of 'mortgage', need I remind you, is 'death pledge'. 'With this Corian, I pledge to work until I die. Longer, if necessary.'

Almost all of the men I've interviewed for this book are worried about money. This would make sense if they had none, but many of them are 'successful'. They might not be rolling in it (although some of them are), but they're certainly doing all right. They're in stable jobs and a decent pay cheque arrives each month, just as it has for years. The problem, then, is not lack of money but the fear of a lack of money. They are at a stage in their lives where they live according to their means, in some cases to the penny. Their lifestyles vary, as do their salaries and their mortgages, but they are all treading the same thin line between outgoings and incomings. None of them has much in reserve. The saving-for-a-rainy-day model of household finance went out with the last housing boom.

'We don't have a safety net,' says one interviewee who has been chasing his tail for twenty minutes in a vain attempt to explain his anxiety. 'We've tried to save up a buffer but something always comes along and wipes it out. If I lost my job, I'd have to find another one in a couple of months or I don't know what would happen.'

What he and his midlife compatriots crave is not more money but more security. And the more they crave it, the more they feel as if they don't have it. At the worst extreme, this becomes a self-fulfilling prophecy. Need turns into anxiety, and anxiety disrupts work, life and that fragile work–life balance.

Researchers have studied the link between money and wellbeing for decades, and the vast majority of them have concluded that cash brings diminishing returns of happiness. Various academics have tried to put a price on happiness in various countries: $75,000 a year in the United States in one study, £70,000 in the United Kingdom in another. Then, in 2018, researchers at a university in Indiana analysed income and wellbeing data from 164 countries. They concluded that Western Europeans reached 'income satiation' – the point where more money ceases to make much of a difference to satisfaction – at £90,000 a year.

That benchmark doesn't account for huge variations in the cost of living across the continent. So I conducted my own much smaller survey in the UK. I asked almost a hundred midlife employees two delicate questions – how much they earned and how happy they were. The results challenge the idea that big salaries guarantee big smiles. On average, the group who earned about £50,000 a year scored themselves 7.3 out of 10 in terms of happiness. The group who earned twice as much rated themselves only 6.1. Two respondents ticked the £250,000-plus box bracket. The first gave himself 9 out of 10 (as, you may think, he bloody well should), but the second managed only 4.

Now, I know the sample size is too small and the questions too general to formulate any grand theory. But the results hint at something that is borne out anecdotally: large earners are by no means guaranteed to be happier than smaller earners. In the 'Any further comments' section of my little survey, the higher earners' responses read like the testimonies in a particularly acrimonious employment tribunal: 'I work very long hours and I'm often away at weekends with little warning,' 'I feel like I could get fired any minute ... we have a high turnover at my company,' 'I have a good salary but I'm expected to bleed for it,' and 'I regret the last promotion ... I took on too much responsibility, but I had no choice.'

Conclusion one: money doesn't equal happiness – your bank balance and your wellbeing are not directly proportional. Conclusion two: well-paid people can feel just as vulnerable as the rest of us, and it makes no difference if that vulnerability is real or perceived. None of this is rocket science. In fact, it's bleeding obvious. Yet, many of us behave as if we've not even considered it. That last guy, the one who regrets his most recent promotion, is typical.

Men who turn down a promotion for the sake of work–life balance, happiness or stability are a much rarer breed. In the course of a year's research, I've found only a handful of them. Why? Partly because saying no would be career suicide. Partly because a promotion epitomises what it means to be a 'success'. It's more status. More stuff. More holidays. More gadgets. Another 'forever' kitchen.

Of course, as I write this, disapprovingly, because our preoccupation with 'success' (still in sarcastic quotes, you'll note) is so clearly a maddening, transient, unsustainable basis for happiness, I know that I am just as guilty as the next man. Status manifests itself perniciously in so much of our lives. It is ingrained from the superhero-cape beginnings right through to the nice-car envy of midlife and beyond. It is how we judge ourselves and others. You may claim you're not like that. You don't judge a book by how many holidays it took last year. But subconsciously, on some level, we're all guilty of trying to keep up with the Joneses. You might twitch your curtains and tut to your wife when the bloke across the road starts cleaning his Tesla for the third time this week, but there is some small part of you that flashes green. Why else would it bother you so much?

When I wrote a column about that weekend in the Corian showroom, those readers who didn't spin off into a frenzied discussion about the relative merits of granite, marble and wood decided I was an idiot. In one strong voice, they told me I shouldn't have wasted money I didn't have. There was no such thing as a 'forever' kitchen, the eighth wonder of the world was compound interest and I would be far happier with laminate surfaces and a cash

ISA. One correspondent had refused a promotion a few years earlier and was now significantly poorer than most of his peers. But, to paraphrase, those peers were now all dropping dead from stress and he was happier than he'd ever been. Hurrah for him.

Another reader took a more philosophical view. 'Whether we carry a wallet worth thirty pounds or three hundred, the amount of money in the wallet is the same,' he wrote. 'Whether we drive a car worth £50,000 or £10,000, we reach the same destination. Whether the house in which we live is three hundred square metres or three thousand, the loneliness is the same. True inner happiness does not come from the material things of this world. Sunlight. Rest. Exercise. Diet. Self-confidence. Friends. Keep them in all stages of life and you will be happy.'

Of course, he is right. In fact, if you followed his advice and ignored everything else in this book, you'd be fine. But that's easier said than done. To understand what we're up against, consider the following examples of human relativism.

In February 1995, students at the Harvard School of Public Health were asked, among other things, to imagine two distinct worlds. In the first, they would each earn $50,000 a year and everyone else would earn $25,000. In the second, their annual income would be a much more comfortable $100,000, but everyone else would clear $200,000. Which world would they prefer? It was a simple choice: you can be relatively well-off but absolutely not, or absolutely well-off but relatively not. You can be the least wealthy person in a wealthy world or the least poor person in a poor world. Entirely predictably, more than half of the students chose the smaller absolute salary. They felt the actual amount they earned was less important than earning more than everyone else.

A year later, psychologists demonstrated the same phenomenon in quite different circumstances. They analysed the facial expressions of medal winners at the 1996 Olympics both immediately after the race and on the podium. In both cases, they found that the bronze medallists were visibly happier than the silver medallists.

When academics at San Francisco State University embarked on a study of judo players at the 2004 Olympics, they identified the same pattern. Eighteen of the twenty-six bronze medallists grinned broadly, but none of the silver medallists could manage even a polite smile. Almost half seemed sad, a third opted for a blank expression and 14 per cent chose outright contempt.*

For me, these windows into human nature are absolutely, not relatively, vital. As I said in Chapter One, we are taught from the moment we crawl – wide-eyed and cherubic – into sentience to compare ourselves to others. We judge our 'success' (still with the air quotes) by benchmarking our achievements and assets against those of everyone else. It is completely and utterly mad that those Harvard students would choose to halve their salaries just to quarter everyone else's, just as it is entirely bonkers that silver medallists are

---

* Since reading these studies, identifying sad/happy silver/bronze medallists has become one of my family's favourite parlour games and also my subtle way, if I do say so myself, of raising my three boys not to be sore losers. It works every time. I guarantee you will never see a smiling silver medallist.

more miserable than bronze medallists. It is mad and bonkers but it is also ingrained in every layer of our experience.

This afternoon, for example, I collected Eli, our youngest, from the after-school drama club he attends each week. He is seven, still young enough to launch into a bit of singing and dancing without the self-consciousness that crushes the Billy-Elliot enthusiasm of older boys. For the first couple of weeks, it took the walk home and a good hour of mind-numbing television for his exuberance to dissipate. He loved the drama unconditionally. In the third week, he was more muted. The steady decline continued in weeks four and five, and now, today, he emerged looking sad. He didn't want to tell me what was wrong, but I continued to probe. Was he hungry? Had there been a fracas with a friend? Had he experienced, as all children do around his age, the sudden and profound realisation that everyone dies? No, no and no. Then, finally, he stopped, his lip wobbled and it all came out. Someone else had won Star Performer of the Week … again.

The teacher had given one pupil the gold medal and left the other twenty-five with the disgruntlement of silver. Before this system had been introduced, in week three, all the children had been in it for the sheer enjoyment of performing. Now, it's a competition with a slim chance of 'success' and a much bigger chance of 'failure'.

So, what's the solution? Well, we shouldn't abandon competition altogether. The everyone's-a-winner sports day is really going a bit far and Olympians are always going to be grumpy when they don't cross the line first. But we shouldn't force children to compete with each other in a misguided attempt to enforce good behaviour in places where it is completely unnecessary ... such as an after-school drama club.

Towards the end of his life, Mark Hanson made copious notes to himself. He was acutely aware that his spiralling thoughts about money and his preoccupation with worst-case scenarios were harmful. He also knew that comparing himself to others only deepened his unhappiness. The notes were his way to remind himself of these facts. At times gently encouraging, at times reproachful, they could have been written by any number of the men I've interviewed for this book. In a ten-point list entitled 'Ways of Reducing Panic about the Future', Mark began with 'Count your blessings', 'Enjoy the now', 'Stop yourself doing what-ifs' and 'You've virtually paid the mortgage on Wilmslow'. For point number nine, he wrote, 'Stop comparing yourself to others – everyone has their own shit'.

To his friends and work colleagues, Mark was an out-going, sociable, driven man – the dictionary definition of 'success'. In his own eyes, he was rather less than that. After disappointing GCSE results, he knuckled down and aced his A-levels. He was the first member of his family to go to university, but never forgot how close he had come to failure. And that fear of failure continued to stalk him as he forged a career in communications. He struggled with low self-esteem and agonised about what might happen if he lost his job. It didn't matter that he'd bounced back with relative ease from two previous redundancies or that his career progression featured far more ladders than snakes.

Mark took his own life in March 2011. He was thirty-six years old, four years into a happy marriage and, by any reasonable measure, on the fast-track to emotional and financial security. He had almost paid off that mortgage on the house in Wilmslow. He and his wife, Clare Francis, both earned decent salaries. They had relocated to Cheshire to be closer to his home town, and they were planning to start a family. But in the end, the physical evidence of Mark's success was insufficient to overcome his own far less generous perception of himself.

In the hard years since Mark's death, Clare has tried to understand what it must be like to suffer with depression and anxiety, working with the mental health charity Mind and as a trustee at the Money and Mental Health Policy Institute. She has tried to answer the unanswerable.

'One thing I have learnt – which, unfortunately, I did not appreciate while he was alive – is just how exhausting it is to cope,' she wrote in a 2017 article for *The Times*. 'Not only did he manage to function and pretend all was fine, even when in a deep depression; he also had an inner battle going on inside his head all day, every day.'

Today, as Clare shares Mark's notes with me, she explains that her goal has always been to help people make different decisions to the one he ultimately made. With hindsight, you can read pain and suffering between the lines. Without hindsight, it is very difficult to distinguish Mark's remonstrations with himself from those of countless other men at his stage of life. He felt the pressures of responsibility, of being successful, of not failing. He had to remind himself of the good things in life. He had to reassure himself that everything was okay. He was his own worst critic ... but aren't we all?

'I called him the squirrel,' says Clare. 'He'd regularly manage to save a few thousand pounds here and there. He had a decent salary – not six figures or anything – but his relationship with money was very different from mine. He didn't have a lot of clothes but those he did have were designer. He could seem extravagant, but then he always took a packed lunch to work and he knew where to find the cheapest coffee in town.' (Greggs, outside Manchester's Piccadilly Station, if you're interested.)

'None of these are necessarily bad habits, but money occupied Mark's mind. He had a bath most nights to help him relax – he had trouble sleeping – and he would call out to ask how much money we owed on our offset mortgage or how much we had in our savings. I used to laugh. I didn't realise the severity of the situation.'

As Clare points out, organisations such as the Money and Mental Health Policy Institute focus on people whose depression is linked to financial difficulty. Such cases – involving problem debt, long-term unemployment and accompanying insolvency – are visible, so they can be addressed. By contrast, Mark had no reason to worry about money so his problems remained hidden, but they were no less debilitating.

'He didn't talk to friends or family,' says Clare. 'He was scared that people would think less of him and would see him as weak. Even with me, he held a lot back. He did this to protect me, he said. He thought I would find it too upsetting.'

This doesn't mean that Mark was not trying to get

well. 'He did so much to try and tackle his illness,' Clare says. 'He had regular counselling and therapy sessions, CBT and acupuncture. He changed his diet and did more exercise. And he was constantly reading, trying to find something that might work for him. In his notes he talks about trying to "crack the code" or "break the code". He believed – or at least hoped – that there would be something that could make him feel better.

'Ultimately, I think that's why he decided to take his life. He was trying to beat his depression, rather than accept it and find a way to manage it. He got to the point where he realised he couldn't beat it. Either that or it all just became too exhausting.'

It is no fun to imagine what Mark went through as his anxiety closed in on him. He was searching for solutions but doing it alone and, alone, the odds were stacked against him. Of course, there are measures we can take to reduce stress and anxiety. Many of the men I've spoken to have done just that. They've found a way through. That way might not be perfect. It might be little more than a distraction, a metaphorical finger-in-the-ears, tra-la-la approach to life. But it gets them through the dark times. Any one of a host of tricks and life hacks might help. You can run through a forest. You can take time for yourself. You can go the full Viktor Frankl and simply choose to be happier.

However ...

Mark's messages to himself are often imbued with this sort of positive thinking, albeit delivered in a less forgiving tone. 'Be happy with yourself and you'll perform well,' he wrote just two months before his death. 'And I did, pretty much – 7/10. Didn't worry I wasn't saying much. Didn't blurt anything out or bottle it. Felt good at the end.'

By urging himself to reframe his thoughts, to stop spiralling, to be kinder to himself, he was following the life-coach playbook. And it didn't work. For a sensitive, thoughtful man like Mark, I wonder if it ever could have done. He was clearly never going to trick himself with a simple distraction technique. That much is evident in his final letter to Clare. 'At the moment, I feel squeezed,' he wrote. 'I could do that job' – he had been offered another rung up the ladder – 'but it would be nothing more than just the next thing achieved. It would give me more cash, more recognition, some highs and some enjoyable days. But it wouldn't solve my problems.

'It would eventually mean moving back to London which in our hearts neither of us wants to do. But what else can I do? Stay up north and get an average job on lower pay? That would create a new set of problems ... feeling that you're struggling for cash, selling yourself short, other people steaming ahead of you.

'You see, this is the shit that goes through my head day in and day out!'

He explained that two factors had stopped him taking his own life. The first was the pain it would cause those he left behind, 'especially you'. But he rationalised that by deciding Clare would be better off without him. The second was shame. 'But I have this shame and low self-esteem while I'm alive so I hope people will focus on everything I achieved.'

Mark had grown up with all the typical patriarchal expectations of the modern man. He had to be successful.

He could not share his feelings for fear of looking weak. If he lost his job, he lost his status and, with it, what it means to be a man. His rational self knew that this was untrue, but, as Clare says, 'His insecurities all too often overpowered him.' Even in his final letter, he was worried about how other people would perceive him.

Mark's notes to himself are deeply upsetting because they are universal. Who doesn't lie awake at night worrying about the mortgage? Who doesn't decide, sporadically, that today is the day to get on top of everything? Who doesn't read the online article 'Ten ways to change your life for the better … NOW!' scoff, then decide you'll have a crack at numbers three and seven?

Back in Chapter Five, I revealed that I had started to compile gratitude lists. I explained that they improved my mood and implied that they could be the route to some sort of catharsis. I sold them like a huckster sells snake oil. But I was exaggerating. I was an unreliable narrator.

The truth is that I wrote them for a while, and told myself they were helping, but after a few days of dubious plate-spinning, the final one was short and entirely insincere. Sitting amid the metaphorical pieces of broken crockery, what I really wanted to write was an ingratitude list. It would have gone something like this:

- I hate my broadband provider and the hours I lost last weekend on the live chat to no one.
- I hate that guy who always leaves his bag on the seat, even when old people are standing.

- I hate not sleeping.
- I hate procrastination.
- I hate that I'm writing bloody gratitude lists to avoid writing this book.
- I hate *The Faraway Tree*.
- I don't like our Corian worktop very much.

That list would have made me feel better. In fact, it has. But as this year of research has gone on, I've felt a pressure to offer solutions. I always knew there was no panacea, no golden bullet to make midlife great, but I had hoped there would be some small salves that I could insert at discreet intervals throughout the book. For me, though, the gratitude list now goes on a very large pile of tried, tested ... and abandoned. The truth is that this is all really hard. We can't new year's resolution our way out of it.

For Mark, his notes were just sticking plasters over a deep wound. His attitude to his own self-worth was set, as it is for all of us, in rigid, formative ways. Without making the radical changes outlined in earlier chapters, without overhauling the way we raise boys and the way we measure success, the mental health statistics will continue to look bleak and there will be more tragic stories to tell.

The great and ridiculous paradox is that those of us who live in richer societies are less happy and more anxious than those who live in poorer societies. To explain this, to understand why Mark felt he was failing while everyone else viewed him as a success, we must first unravel how we evaluate ourselves and others. Stick Mark's ninth point on the fridge: 'Stop comparing yourself to others – everyone has their own shit'.

Clare has turned her grief into a laudable determination to help other sufferers. She relives her own darkest days in her efforts to raise awareness. But she accepts that some questions will never be answered. 'I'll always wonder if things might have been different if Mark had been able to talk to a friend or tell someone at work,' she says.

If onlys are the cruellest aspect for those left behind. If only Mark had talked to a friend. If only men talked more in general. That's step one. But step two – what do we do if and when men open up? – is more challenging. When men have dropped their guard in interviews, I've found myself reaching for solutions. I want to magic wand their problems away. To the friend with a heart problem, still commuting to the job he hates: 'Come on, mate, stop getting on that train. Take some time off. Reassess.' To the financial consultant who hides in the bath and likens his four-hour commute to a psychological waterboarding: 'Come on, mate, stop hiding in the bath. Talk to your wife. Change jobs.' To Mark: 'Come on, mate, be kinder to yourself.'

All of these quick and easy solutions go in the same box as jogging, analogue living, yoga, meditation and not checking your emails in the evenings. They treat the symptoms, not the disease. They are to midlife misery what Nurofen is to backache. Fine in the short term but not the same as ten sessions with an osteopath and a complete rethink on posture.

In more pessimistic moments, I feel like it is already too late for the current crop of midlifers. We're too indoctrinated in the outdated, old-fashioned ways of man. With guidance and an urgent rethink, our sons have a chance to live different, happier lives, but we've missed the boat. We'll just have to stick with the Nurofen and the whisky and wait for the happiness curve to turn upwards again, as magically it does, in older age.

In more optimistic moments, I think it's not quite that bad. Happiness is still up for grabs.

Our generation has witnessed, and is still witnessing, monumental shifts in how men and women coexist. The need to rectify the great inequality served up to women since the dawn of time has driven those changes, but, although the changing role of women has changed the role of men too, we haven't liked to talk about it. Too controversial. Too risky. Might be cast as anti-feminist or anti-equality or just plain sexist. Sensible men, those who know what's good for them, have just ploughed on, wordlessly navigating the choppy seas between traditional, stoic manliness and modern, hands-on, emotionally available manliness. Less sensible men have behaved as if they are under attack, climbing cranes in Spiderman costumes and filling Incel message boards with frustrated bile about positive discrimination and political correctness gone mad.

The good news is that we're finally reaching a point where it's okay to talk about what it means to be a man. This doesn't need to be an aggressive conversation. We don't need to fight for our rights or engage in a battle of the sexes. As we continue to move, albeit sluggishly, towards economic equality, we are also approaching the next stage of the Gender Transition Model – where men not only want but have emotional equality. Stoicism be damned.

Back when I was exaggerating the beneficial effects of

my gratitude lists, I also introduced you to Dr Ben Sinclair, who claims that the sight of a deer during his morning run sustains him through the rest of the day. When I mentioned this to my wife, who is much further down the meditative road than I am, she pointed out that this is not as simple as it seems. Merely subduing negative thoughts while you're in the woods is hard enough. Reaching the point where you can fully appreciate the flora or fauna around you is even harder. And extrapolating that appreciation into day-long sustenance is black-belt mindfulness.

'Pleasure is always derived from something outside you, whereas joy arises from within,' writes Eckhart Tolle, the best-selling (not that he cares about that sort of external validation) author of *The Power of Now*. 'The primary cause of unhappiness is never the situation but the thought about it. Be aware of the thoughts you are thinking. Separate them from the situation, which is always neutral. It is as it is.'

The urge to measure ourselves against others is tightly woven into the fabric of our lives, but it creates needless unhappiness. Don't think about that the next time you go for a walk in the woods. Don't think about anything except for the tree or the deer or the woodlouse you encounter. And don't think about how lucky the woodlouse is because he doesn't have a mortgage and lives in the moment. Don't envy a bloody woodlouse, for goodness' sake. He doesn't have Corian worktops. Damn.

CHAPTER NINE

Men and . . . happiness

Down a pot-holed lane in East Sussex, around the neatly tended vegetable patches of the Little Tinkers Nursery, turn left at the chickens, right at the ducks, and you'll find a shed. At eleven o'clock every Thursday morning, that shed will be full of twelve old men.

On the face of it, these men have all been put – or have put themselves – out to pasture. They have retired or taken redundancy or just decided to step off the carousel. Some of them chose the precise moment of their departure. For others, there was less control. A health scare or a restructuring or one Sisyphean task or bamboozling technological upgrade too many and that was it. The final P45. Game over.

Regardless of the circumstances, all of these men have survived that great challenge – to hang up their work boots and not immediately drop dead. For that is what we all face at the end of decades of toil – a significantly elevated chance of kicking the bucket. Statistically, the two most dangerous years of your life are the year you are born and the year you retire.

This particular shed is about as far from a pasture full of old nags as you are likely to get. For starters, there are doughnuts and the conversation is bright and breezy. Why wouldn't it be? Surely this is every man's dream – a shed full of tools, a workbench, friends and those doughnuts. Set up last year, it is now one of more than five hundred Men's Sheds across the UK – much-needed facilities for men who can't join the Women's Institute and can't face the knit-and-natter mornings at the local community centre.

Each week, the 'shedders' meet up and make stuff. Their first project was to build the shed itself. Then they made a swanky crib for the local Nativity display. Now, as they finalise the plans for a larger shed in an adjacent field, they are turning out beautiful bird boxes and wooden bowls for sale in the local market. But, judging by today, this is not the shed's primary purpose. The main activity I witness is chat ... with, don't forget, doughnuts.

'There's a high rate of depression, loneliness and feelings of isolation among retired men,' says Peter Brock, the former electrical engineer who founded the shed. 'Unlike their female counterparts, they struggle to engage socially with others and adapt to retirement. Our shed is a community space for men to connect, converse and create. It reduces isolation and, most importantly, it's fun.'

In the early months, Peter and membership secretary Nic used their local market stall to drum up new recruits.

'You'd be surprised at the number of women who came up to the stall dragging their husbands behind them,' says Peter. 'They say, "Will you take him?" and we say, "Yes, we'll take him." One guy was cajoled to come and left after twenty minutes. But he was the only one who didn't stay. I think his wife must have been waiting in the car park.'

The reluctance is understandable. Socialising can be anathema to men who have witnessed the gradual shrinking of friendship groups over decades. Weekly all-nighters become monthly nights out, become, by middle age, much-postponed, little-anticipated biannual obligations.

Studies show that men talk less as we get older. In extreme cases, we withdraw altogether, favouring a hermetic existence to anything approaching a social life. In the squeezed middle years, we do little more than work, parent and sleep. When the kids are old enough, we just work and sleep. So what do we do when we retire? We can't sleep all the time. Meeting up once a week in a shed might not sound particularly glamorous, but it is a community, a rebuilding of life outside work and family.

'When we started, people were a bit shy and backed off,' says Peter, to murmurs of agreement. 'But as we've got together more, we talk a lot more, we take the mickey more, we go out, we go to the pub, we go out for breakfast. It's been a complete transformation and it happened on its own, which is fantastic.'

I ask all the men to think back over their lives and consider what they should have done differently. This is my clumsy attempt to glean the wisdom of the elders, but the first man to answer insists he would change nothing. 'I'm perfectly happy with the way my life went,' says Phil. 'I worked far too hard but now I get the benefits.'

Graham agrees. He took steps in his working life to ensure he had a reasonably comfortable retirement, he says. Very quickly, a consensus is reached: it's worth sacrificing midlife happiness for a rosy old age. But then Graham tells me about his ex-wife's father, who ran a successful architectural business. 'His ultimate aim was to buy a Rover 90,' says Graham. 'He retired and within a year he'd got his Rover and he'd died.'

This unleashes a chorus of anecdotes about men working hard, then dropping dead.

'When I first started working,' says Peter, 'there were senior guys in the head office hanging on for bigger pensions. They were so focused on work that they had nothing else. It was so sad. They worked all that time and then, three months into retirement, they've painted the house, done the garden and run out of things to do. A lot of them passed away.'

Ken was sixty-two when he chucked in his work towel. 'It sounds really silly for a librarian to say this, but I was managing large budgets and it was increasingly stressful,' he says. 'A few warning signs kicked in and I knew that my mental health was suffering. I was asked to restructure a load of services with a budget two-thirds too small and that was the straw that broke the camel's back.' He firmly believes that you need interests in life besides work, but these must be chosen wisely. As a school governor, he supervised a large, multi-year building project, but, 'It was really just replicating what I did at work, which just added pressure. Arguably, I would have been better off doing something practical.'

'You need a passion,' suggests Nic. 'My advice is to pick one that isn't too expensive. It doesn't matter what it is as long as you make time for it. I was talking to a guy about the shed last week and he told me that he had cultivated an interest in tools for thirty years. He had even written a book about it. I asked him what tools he was interested in. He said, "Adjustable spanners."'

'I've had a passion for woodwork since I was a kid,' says Mick. 'I had three kids and I don't know where the eighties went, but that didn't stop me from keeping a workshop. I always had things going on besides work. I went fishing, I played in a band. Those things went away a bit when I had kids, but they come back again in later life.'

At this point Ron – a retired draughtsman and, at eighty-seven, the second-oldest duffer in the oil-fire-heated room – points at a wall of framed tapestries and says, 'That's been my passion for twenty-five years. Each one of those has thirteen thousand cross-stitches. I started one winter and I've been *hooked* ever since.' Boom, boom.

So, there you have it. The answers to life, the universe and everything are cross-stitching, adjustable spanners and woodwork. Or work hard, but not for ever, and get out when the going's good. Or negotiate a four-day week (which changed Nic's life). Or work from home (which changed Peter's). Or – as is plain to see in all these marvellous men in their shed – cherish your friendships.

Midlife is more of a tightrope walk than it has ever been, so the urge is to prioritise what seems most important – financial security, the children, the career, the work–life balance, the future. 'Men today live to work rather than work to live,' says the other Peter in the shed, who is ninety-two years old, so we should listen. What is just as important is community, he says. What is more important is passion.

This is why I want to finish this book with the story of a man who prioritises passion above all else. I am not the first person to interview Steve Feltham. Every now and again, a news producer or a journalist will head up to the Scottish Highlands to seek out his converted mobile library van. Why? Because they're after a quirky story. Because that van sits on the southern shore of Loch Ness. And because Steve Feltham is the Nessie Hunter. He's been hunting for the Loch Ness monster for almost thirty years. It's definitely a quirky story.

When I first got in touch, I told him I wasn't interested in the monster hunting itself. I wanted to discuss the how and why, rather than the what. How had he ended up spending most of his adult life parked up on a remote beach in Scotland? How had he swerved one way when the rest of us swerve the other? Why wasn't he an accountant with a mortgage and a miserable commute?

At that stage, it was hard to know if he would tell me anything useful. Nine times out of ten, the person at the centre of a quirky human-interest story is not particularly instructive. But the more we talked, the more I realised that Steve is not completely bonkers. On the contrary, he may well have found what is, for him at least, the perfect way to live his life.

Steve's passion for Loch Ness and its purported monster began on a family holiday when he was seven. His young mind, still open to adventure, magic and make-believe, was gripped by the mystery. Later holidays did nothing to extinguish his enthusiasm. Nor did adolescence or adulthood. For the first ten years of his working life, he progressed through a variety of jobs in his native Dorset. He was a potter, then a bookbinder, then a graphic artist. But he continued to make regular pilgrimages to the loch. 'I'd come up and pitch a tent on the side of the loch,' he says. 'I'd spend two weeks contemplating Loch Ness and its mystery and taking the opportunity to think about things. The euphoria that I would take back home was obvious. All my friends could see it.'

At twenty-five, Steve was on the verge of settling down. He had bought a house with his girlfriend and had gone into partnership with his dad, installing burglar alarms in the Bournemouth area. This was the time to pack away all thoughts of the monster and start chipping away at the mortgage, but Steve decided to take a different path.

'Bournemouth has a huge retired population and they're the first people to want a burglar alarm because they are the most paranoid,' he says. 'Every day in a different house, I was having a conversation with these retired people and every single one of them said, "When I was your age, I wish I'd ... " They were full of regret about lost dreams and I just felt that weight. I could see that I would be there one day, looking back, wishing I'd had the courage ... And all the time, Loch Ness was calling.'

Those ghosts of Christmas future left Steve in turmoil, so

he headed off to the loch – 'the best three weeks of my life so far' – to find some answers. Back home, with the euphoria ebbing away, he found himself sitting at a friend's kitchen table in the small hours. Several beers in, he announced that he was going to immerse himself fully in the Loch Ness mystery. 'We all have big ideas after a few beers, but I was still convinced the next morning. I had a choice between predictability and unpredictability. Society, the powers that be, portray unpredictability as a fearful thing. They don't want everyone jumping in vans and escaping the nine to five. But I'm living proof that if you wholeheartedly commit yourself to whatever it is you want to do, it makes your heart sing.'

The twenty-five-year-old Steve never would have predicted that he would still be up here twenty-nine years later, still combing the shores, still staring out across the water. But as he describes his day-to-day routine, the life he's chosen seems less surprising. He has no alarm clock. He wakes up early on long summer days and late in the winter. The first thing he does each morning is pull back the curtain to decide if he'll head outside or stay inside. After that, it's all quite serendipitous. He might spend some time making the Nessie models he sells to passing tourists. He might explore a different section of the loch. Or he might go out in his boat and retrieve a piece of driftwood masquerading as the monster. There are slow periods and fast periods, but he enjoys them all.

'All of the documentary makers who have come like to portray me as this tragic, wifeless freak, living his hermit life on the side of the loch and never turning his back on the water. But when they do a wide shot of my van, if they would just pan back a fraction more, you'd see a Mr Whippy ice-cream van. And two hundred yards over there are the doors to the pub. It's a long way from a hermit's existence, but that's the way the media choose to portray me.

'They want to give the impression that I live this frugal existence for the sake of the mystery, but I don't feel like I've given up anything. I feel like I've gained massively. The only thing I don't have is a bathtub, but, you know, I've got the biggest loch in Scotland outside my front door. Success shouldn't be measured financially. Success is spending enough time doing the things you love.'

Steve jokes that he retired at twenty-eight – the age when he settled permanently by the loch. He is now fifty-six. 'I'm at an age when life options begin to diminish,' he says. 'There aren't so many unpredictable adventures. But, for me, they're coming bigger and faster than ever. And it all comes about through sitting in the one place, looking at the one body of water, and waiting to see what happens.'

As Steve makes his Nessie models, he compares himself to a Greek fisherman with his worry beads. His is a meditative life, as much about living in the moment and finding joy in simple things as it is about what might be swimming beneath the surface. His favourite time of day, when he is awake that late, is one or two in the morning. 'It doesn't matter if it's a calm, moonlit night or if it's blowing a gale,' he says. 'I stand on my decking and the breeze comes off the water. The rain and wind whip straight off the loch and hit me. I feel the freedom I felt when I first came here at the age of seven. Sometimes that breeze feels like it goes into my chest and comes out the top of my head like a column of white light . . . of absolute, unbelievable luck.'

Perhaps the greatest challenge we all face, and certainly something I've struggled with while writing this book, is how to quell the mind. The insistent voice in your head that lists all the things you should be worrying about on an unremitting loop is the enemy of creativity and happiness. Some people try to silence it with meditation apps, others do yoga, others still run marathons. Steve has managed to distil his solution into a breeze coming off the water in the middle of the night. He's not crazy. He's bordering on transcendental. I don't even think his epic, life-long attempt to solve the mystery of the Loch Ness monster is the main reason he's here. It's the official reason, sure, but what really motivates him is his appreciation of what he has. The rest of us might think he has very little, but he knows he's one of the richest men on the planet.

When tourists ask him, as they always do, if he has seen the monster, he reports one brief sighting fifteen years ago – 'Something went through the bay at the other end of the loch like a torpedo.' When I ask if he is content with that, his answer is fascinating. 'If I had a proper ten-minute sighting of something out here and had to describe that four hundred times a day, I'm pretty sure that I would quickly go back to saying, "Nah. I haven't seen it yet." I'm not here to convince the world that the Loch Ness monster is real. I wouldn't mind if I worked out exactly what was going on and decided not to bother telling the rest of the world. If I reach my deathbed and the mystery hasn't been solved, I would not think that my life had been wasted. I have filled my heart with joy and I have had the greatest adventure I possibly could have had. That is enough.'

I'm thinking of making a fridge magnet with 'That is enough' printed on it.

Looking back across each chapter of this book – each stage of a man's life – the common denominator is that there are always goals. Boys and exams. Young men and careers. Dads and work–life balance. We judge ourselves on how close we are to achieving these goals. What would happen if we stopped? Would the whole edifice of life come crashing down if we worried a little less about those goals and focused a little more on just enjoying the moment? Possibly. Those men at the start of the book who are afraid even to consider their own happiness lest their finely balanced lives spin out of control certainly think so. But this is not a happy way to live. At best, they will make it through to the greener-grass, rocking-chair bliss of the third age. At worst, like Mark Hanson, they won't.

It would be terrible if we all followed in Steve's footsteps. For a start, Loch Ness would be ruined. But there is a lesson in how he lives his life. Or a reminder. We all start out as dreamers – children with big plans involving spaceships, magic and monsters – and then, through the collective efforts of school, society and our own inner critic, we grow up and get real. We get caught up in the process. Our room for manoeuvre shrinks. Common sense replaces passion. Planning for the future replaces living every day like our hair is on fire. It doesn't have to be that way. Or at least it doesn't have to be that way entirely. If Steve can find joy, come rain or very occasional shine, on his decking in the frigid far north of Scotland, we can all find it.

There is no doubt that our generation is under great strain. Technology has made our lives harder, not easier. Employment is more precarious and therefore more stressful than it has been since the 1930s. House prices have increased tenfold, while salaries have barely kept pace with inflation. Our mental health is deteriorating. Our anxiety levels are rising. We are always connected but rarely connect. We are in a state of flux – one manly foot in the old patriarchy, the other in modern equality. And I'm writing this as the whole world is kicked off its axis by coronavirus, so who knows where we'll be by the time you read it?

And yet, this book has given me the time and opportunity – for the first time in my life – to consider what it really means to be a man in the twenty-first century. I have been able to step off the hamster's wheel for a few months (at least on Fridays, Saturdays and Sundays). That, in itself, has been a quite profound experience. It is easy to get wrapped up in our own problems. The constant demands of work and home can leave us living an entirely reactive existence, lurching from one challenge to the next. What I've learnt is that breaking free is relatively simple. You don't have to move to Loch Ness on the pretext of searching for monsters. You don't have to wait until you're seventy and making bird boxes in a shed. It can start with a few minutes in the garden each morning. Or looking up an old friend. Or putting your name down for orienteering or origami (or something that doesn't start with 'or . . .'). It can start by caring a little less about stuff that doesn't matter.

It's interesting – as well as terrifying – to watch the world grind to a halt in this pandemic. It has taken a crisis of an unprecedented magnitude to force us to pause. Perhaps everything will return to normal when it's all over. Perhaps we'll return to our rushed, fragmented, individual lives. Perhaps there will be excitable queues outside the Apple Store and Ryanair will fill the skies and Italians will stop singing from their balconies. Perhaps it will be like nothing ever happened, and the only long-term effect will be a residual obsession with handwashing.

Then again, there might be a more profound transformation. It is at least a remote possibility that things will change a bit. Success might no longer be measured entirely by how much stuff you have. A successful man might be a happy man. Or a generous man. Or a passionate man. Or just a man who listened to his heart, not his head, for a few minutes each day.

And that would be a good thing.

Acknowledgements

Thank you to the team at Piatkus – my editor Zoe Bohm, Jillian Stewart, Jo Wickham and Aimee Kitson – all of whom have worked skilfully and thoughtfully on a whole book about how hard things can be for men – men! – without once losing patience. Or maybe they did – it's harder to tell over Zoom. Thank you also to Nico Taylor for a cover that does not feature a cigarette butt stubbed out on a wedding cake.

Thank you to my agent Euan Thorneycroft who, despite suffering his own midlife angst in the form of a full-on beard, continues to remain calm and optimistic at just the right times.

Thank you to my colleagues, particularly Eleanor Mills and Krissi Murison, who allowed/encouraged my midlife crisis to play out in the pages of the *Sunday Times Magazine*. Very healthy.

And thank you to Harriet, my wife and teammate in everything. Only once – okay, three times – did she point out the irony of writing a chapter about hands-on parenting while not doing nearly enough hands-on parenting. She is always the first person on my gratitude list. She is never on my ingratitude list.

And thank you to all the men who agreed to talk so openly and honestly. Awkward, wasn't it? But we got there.